Cybersecurity

A Simple Beginner's Guide to Cybersecurity, Computer Networks and Protecting Oneself from Hacking in the Form of Phishing, Malware, Ransomware, and Social Engineering

Contents

Introduction

The Internet may be the most important invention of the twenty-first century, and it affects people's lives daily in more ways than they realize. Everything has changed since the invention of the Internet—the way you communicate, play games, shop, work, listen to music, watch movies, pay bills, order food, and even the way you make friends. Think of anything you want, and there is probably a mobile or web-based app for it.

The Internet has made people's lives very comfortable. You do not need to stand in a queue or write a check to pay a bill anymore. You can just get done it at the click of some buttons. Technology has advanced to such an extent that millions of devices are capable of connecting to the Internet—most don't need to be connected to your computer. There are smartphones, tablets, etc., through which you can stay connected to your friends and even work whenever you want.

The Internet has not only simplified things but also made them cost-effective due to how it is used not only by the rich but all classes in society. In the past, people had to think very hard before making international calls because of the charges imposed by telecom providers. Today, you can use the Internet to make standard and video calls at great rates, even free in some cases, anywhere in the world.

The Internet has also changed the adoption rate of traditional devices like television, as people now prefer to watch everything through a subscription model on the Internet. People do not use a mobile phone just to make calls anymore, but tons of other activities, such as watching a movie, booking tickets online, etc. The Internet has even made it possible to work from home, which is convenient for parents as they can keep a watch over toddlers at the same time. In other words, people have become closer since the arrival of the Internet.

However, the Internet has made way for new kinds of crime, too, known as cybercrimes. While the Internet became the "in place" for people to hang out and socialize, it also offered cybercriminals massive opportunities. Criminals realized that with everything going digital, they also needed to adapt and go digital too. It did not take them much time to understand that the entire world uses the utilities provided by the Internet for activities such as shopping, banking, ordering food, etc., and that all of these have a common twist—financial transactions over digital media. Billions of dollars, British pounds, and thousands of other currencies are moved around via the Internet these days, every day, and that is a huge attraction to criminals, providing an alternative way for them to commit their crimes.

A thief does not need to walk into a bank anymore to steal money; it can be done over the Internet. This led to the arrival of cybercriminals who commit crimes over the Internet known as cybercrimes. In this book, you will learn about all kinds of cybercrimes and how cybercriminals implement them.

If there is a law in the real world to keep a watch over criminal activity, there are processes in the digital world to keep cybercrimes under control. Cybersecurity is a hot term used on the Internet, and that is what this book is all about. You will learn about the various ways through which you can use cybersecurity to counter cybercrimes.

By the end of the book, you will also have read about security testing and the careers you can have for yourself in the cybersecurity domain if you are an aspiring student or looking to switch your field from your current profession. This book will open your eyes to new possibilities and bring out the digital version of Sherlock Holmes residing within you.

Chapter One: Cybersecurity and Why It's Important

What is Cybersecurity?

Cybersecurity, also known as information security, is defined as the process of ensuring ICA of information, where I stands for Integrity, C stands for Confidentiality, and A stands for Availability. Cybersecurity comprises a set of relevant tools, approaches toward risk management, training, technologies, and methods to protect the information, networks, programs, and devices against attacks and unauthorized access.

The following entities are part of the cybersecurity process.

People

People are part of a system. It could be a university or an organization or another institution. During their tenure with an institution, people should understand and comply with the basic principles of data security, such as using strong passwords, being alert about email attachments, and doing data backups.

Processes

Organizations need to have certain frameworks in place to tackle cyberattacks, both attempted and successful ones. If an organization has even one well-respected framework, it can guide them in times of a cyberattack. A framework will help them identify the attacker, protect all systems, be response-ready for threats, and quickly recover in case of successful attacks.

Technology

Without technology, organizations would not have the necessary tools for computer security to protect themselves against cyberattacks. There are three main entities to protect: personal end-point devices—such as smart devices, computers, and routers—the network, and the cloud. The common technologies used to protect these entities include firewalls, DNS filters, anti-malware solutions, antivirus solutions, and email security solutions.

Why is Cybersecurity Important?

Today, the world depends on technology more than it ever did in past decades. This has resulted in a huge surge in the creation of digital data. Data is stored on computers by individuals, businesses, government agencies, etc., and daily transferred to other computers over a network. There are loopholes and vulnerabilities in computers and their underlying systems. These can be exploited by an attacker, which leads to the downfall of an organization. This is why cybersecurity is vital.

A breach in the system that allows an attacker access can have far-reaching consequences. The leak of customer data can affect the organization's reputation and lead to a loss of trust with partners and customers. Theft of software source code can cost the organization a competitive advantage over its rivals. Additionally, a data breach can cause revenue losses due to data protection practices being non-compliant.

On average, a data breach can cost an organization up to USD 3.6 million. Moreover, high-profile data breaches make it into the news headlines like wildfire resulting in a hit on a company's reputation. This is why organizations need to implement a strong and powerful approach to cybersecurity.

Cybersecurity Scenarios

This section discusses the need for information security. You will go through a few common scenarios in which cybersecurity is used in the world today.

Scenario for Organizations

Try to picture an organization with all the latest IT equipment to cater to all their digital needs for their business to function smoothly. It is critical for this IT infrastructure to be up and running around the clock. The organization also needs to ensure that the identity of the data, network, equipment, and products are secured, except for public-access network and data identities. However, the public data itself must still be encrypted and secured. All organizations have gone digital, and therefore there is a mix of various technologies working together to drive the goals and objectives of an organization. Digitization also extends the boundaries of an organization, thereby increasing their connectivity. The connectivity is, of course, an advantage today but can be harmful to the organization.

Three macro aspects define digitization and connectivity:

- Identity – This is an aspect through which users can interact.
- Data – This is data related to the user, business, system, or customer.
- Network – This is the part where everyone is connected and restricted via access levels.

These three macro entities are connected via equipment, software, and business processes. As already mentioned, an organization controls the level of access a user may have to create, view, or modify data via access developed for an identity. Additionally, data—whether it is in rest or motion—also needs to be secured. And finally, it goes without saying that the network perimeter for this infrastructure, whether it is in a physical form or on the cloud, requires security.

The Scenario Where Everything is Moving to the Cloud

What is the cloud? A cloud is a common space on the Internet where all your data can be stored instead of storing it locally. Most organizations are rapidly moving all their data to the cloud. This happens because cloud-based servers offer better computing power, and the cost of storing data on the cloud is less than storing it locally. Another benefit of cloud-based infrastructure is that it is scalable. This means that its parameters such as RAM, computing power, and disk space can be expanded on the go.

With the Internet, the world is getting smaller, and organizations have started collaborating on a global scale, and cloud computing is to be credited for this. Gone are the days when employees would sit in an office and work. Today, employees prefer working out of remote locations, thereby eliminating the need for a physical office. Cloud infrastructure also takes away the burden on local IT teams to constantly keep a watch for software and hardware upgrades.

Cloud infrastructure has definitely brought in a new era of more speed, control, accuracy, power, and availability, but many security risks also accompany it. Cloud infrastructure is no different vis-à-vis security, and disasters can happen if that infrastructure is not secured properly. The biggest advantage of cloud infrastructure is that an organization does not have to own or maintain infrastructure. However, the boon is accompanied by concerns such as how do you secure it? Who has access to the data present in the cloud? How do you keep the cloud compliant with government regulations such as PCI or GDPR?

The service provider's business model also governs the disaster recovery policy around cloud infrastructure, and therefore an organization needs to be up to date on this. The organization does not have any say in where the service provider's data center is located. There are several other risks and challenges to using cloud infrastructure, which will be discussed in the next few chapters.

Cybersecurity Terminology

Several terms used throughout this book relate to the cybersecurity domain. It is important to cover these terms in the first chapter so that you are familiar with them when they start making subsequent appearances. These terms are related to all the devices you use today, the software on those devices, the network infrastructure the devices are connected to, and so on. You will now go through these terms individually.

Cloud

The Internet is made up of clouds—and not the ones in the sky. Cloud computing is a technology that allows a user to access their files from anywhere in the world. Cloud is a network of computers that store data that can be accessed by a smart device remotely. The most common example of a cloud is your emails. They are stored on a distributed set of computers on the Internet, and you get to access them from anywhere as long as you have the required credentials. Another example would be something like a Spotify playlist that you have created using your mobile phone, but you still get to access the same playlist from another device like a laptop when you log in using the same account.

Software

The software can be defined as instructions that tell a computer what to do. These instructions are put into a package known as software, which a user can install and start using. One of the most common software examples is Microsoft Office, which is used to create documents, presentations, etc. Your smartphone apps are also software that you use for various purposes. For example, WhatsApp messenger is the most common app used to send messages.

Domain

A domain is a parent for child devices that are interconnected, such as computers, smartphones, printers, etc. For example, all the computers at a workplace are a part of a domain belonging to the organization. There are policies defined in the domain's framework that govern the type of access that the devices will have under that domain.

IP Address

An IP address is a digital address assigned to a smart device over a network, which can be a local network or the Internet. Every device connected to a network is associated with an IP address. That IP address is used by other devices to locate and communicate with each other.

Virtual Private Network (VPN)

A virtual private network is a network over which you can be anonymous. You get assigned an IP belonging to a different region, and all your actions over the Internet are logged via that IP, thus keeping your original IP hidden. VPN applications also encrypt the traffic for you so that the Internet Service Provider or the government cannot track your activities online. VPNs are also used by organizations to keep you connected to the office network if you want to access the office network from outside. This has gained a lot of popularity in recent times as it helps a person work from home or remotely.

Exploit

An exploit is defined as a malicious piece of code that can be used to take advantage of a vulnerability or loophole in a computer or a server. Viruses, Trojans, Botnets, etc., are all used to execute an exploit in a target system.

Breach

The moment when an attacker takes advantage of a system's vulnerability, and gains access, is known as a breach.

Firewall

The technology used to create rules for a system, so incoming and outgoing traffic can be filtered, is known as a firewall. Firewalls can be implemented using both hardware and software.

Malware

Malware is a broad term or an umbrella that includes any malicious software that can harm a computer. The most common types of malware are viruses, worms, Trojans, ransomware, etc.

Virus

A virus is defined as malware that can harm certain programs on a computer. It can further replicate itself and spread over multiple files and computer networks. It needs a host file and cannot execute by itself. Viruses were known to affect only software, but they have evolved in recent years even to cause physical damage to hardware.

Ransomware

Ransomware is a type of malware that will encrypt all the data on your computer and prevent you from accessing it. The attacker who deployed the ransomware will leave an application where you make a payment to them, after which the files will automatically be decrypted. In 2017, a ransomware known as WannaCry infected all Windows-based machines.

Trojan Horse

A Trojan horse is like a virus, but it does not execute by itself. It is usually masked and lies under a file, which may be important to a user. For example, a user may receive a PDF with the content they were expecting, but at the same time, clicking on that PDF triggers a malicious script. This implementation is known as a Trojan horse.

Worm

A worm is a piece of malicious code that is capable of replicating itself over a network. It may not necessarily infect a file like a virus does, but it can do something annoying like consuming the network bandwidth and denying the bandwidth to the user.

Bot or Botnet

A Bot is a malicious application that can be planted over a network of computers, allowing an attacker to remotely take control of the complete network. The collection of computers on which the bots are planted is called a botnet. The botnet is controlled by an attacker who is known as bot herder.

DDoS

DDoS stands for Distributed Denial of Service and is a form of cyberattack. The motive of a DDoS attack is to flood a network with malicious traffic so that genuine requests for a website cannot be accommodated in the bandwidth. DDoS attacks are often executed by implementing botnets.

Phishing and Spear Phishing

This is a technique that is used by attackers to retrieve information. The most common example of this is emails sent to unsuspecting users, which may seem legit but will have links redirecting you to something else. For example, if you have an account with Citibank, the sender of the email will have an email address like something@citibanks.com, adding an extra S. An innocent user may believe it to be legit and may end up clicking on a link they are not supposed to. These links can often ask you to enter your account details and even login passwords that will be recorded by the attacker.

Encryption

The process of encoding data using a known algorithm so that no one can access it, except someone with a decoding key, is called encryption.

Bring Your Own Device (BYOD)

This is a policy implemented by many organizations that suggests that employees can use their personal devices for business. A BYOD policy will have access restrictions concerning whether the personal device can connect to the corporate network or not.

Penetration Testing

Penetration testing—also known as a pen-test—is the process of using attacking tools and techniques to review the security of an organization's infrastructure. Internal teams or external experts are hired to conduct the test to discover vulnerabilities in the organization's infrastructure so that they can be fixed before encountering a real attack.

Clickjacking

This is an attack that tricks the user into clicking on a link or button, which looks genuine but has malicious scripts embedded in it.

This book has only covered the tip of the iceberg for cybersecurity terminology, but this will serve as a launchpad to better understanding.

History of Cyberattacks

In this section, you will go through the most well-known cyberattacks in history. Cyberspace is an open community where everyone is connected and can reach anyone irrespective of time or distance. It may be called a way of life today, but if not used with care, it has consequences. There are notorious people in the world who use cyberspace to attack websites belonging to banks, social media that contains a gold mine of user information, and even governments. Here are a few modern cyberattacks.

The SpamHaus Project

SpamHaus is a public service on the Internet that helps filter out spam emails based on their content or the reputation of their origin. The attack on SpamHaus is considered to be the biggest cyberattack in history where home and business broadband router owners were targeted. The attackers gained control over these routers, and all these users became involuntary participants of the attack. Millions of email service providers use SpamHaus to filter out spam emails from the Internet. On March 18, 2013, SpamHaus had blacklisted a company called Cyberbunker, which led to losses for the company. Cyberbunker and other hosting companies retaliated to this by hiring hackers who deployed botnets by exploiting broadband routers to shut down the SpamHaus network.

Sony Playstation

In 2011, information such as credit card details and user information was stolen from 77 million users by a group of hackers. This cost Sony around USD two billion in damages. Another pain point for the company happened when hackers were continuously able to access the Sony network using the login details of gamers even when the company was trying to fix the issue. This whole attack lasted for twenty-four days.

PayPal

In December 2010, PayPal became a victim of a cyberattack. This happened immediately after PayPal had blocked the account of WikiLeaks for fundraising, citing violation of PayPal's acceptable usage policy. Multiple users boycotted PayPal because of this event, and many hackers started targeting PayPal.

Canadian Government Hacking

In February 2011, the Canadian government disclosed via multiple news channels that they had become victim to hacking conducted from IPs that were traced back to China. The attackers were able to access three departments of the Canadian government and stole data from those departments. The attack was eventually stopped by cutting off Internet access to these three departments, putting a full stop to the transmission of data to China.

4chan

4chan is an English language based website used for posting pictures and discussing Japanese anime and manga. It was launched in October 2003 by a fifteen-year-old New York student named Christopher Poole. The users were allowed to post anonymously, which served as a drawback for the website. A user, Hal Turner, claimed he was the target of DDoS attacks and prank phone calls made to his radio show in 2006. In 2008, an anonymous 4chan user hacked the private Yahoo mail account of Sarah Palin, a candidate for vice-presidential elections.

Citigroup

Citigroup is one of the largest financial institutions in the world. On its own, this was enough incentive for notorious attackers to target their network as it had a lot of sensitive and valuable information flowing through it daily. An attack in 2011 on the Citigroup network led to customer information, such as contact details and account information, being stolen from more than 200,000 customers. The company suffered monetary damage of USD 2.7 million due to this attack.

Michael Calce

In 2000, a fifteen-year-old boy named Michael Calce, popularly known as "Mafiaboy" in cyberspace, gained the spotlight for hacking high-profile companies such as computer giant Dell, Fifa.com, Yahoo, Amazon, CNN, and eBay, causing damage worth USD 1.2 billion. He also attacked nine out of thirteen root name servers of the Internet domain space. Being a juvenile, Calce got away with only eight months of open custody, a year of probation, and a small fine. He was also not allowed to own any Internet-powered device by the Montreal Youth Court for eight months.

Chapter Two: Cyberattacks and 10 Types of Cyber Hackers

The Internet that you know today came into existence in the 1960s, and it was only accessible to a few scientists, researchers, and the Defense Departments at that time. However, the user base for the Internet has evolved exponentially ever since. In the initial days, a cybercrime was described as physical damage to a computer and its infrastructure. This definition of cybercrime changed in the 1980s to include using a virus that would cause a computer to malfunction.

The effect of cybercrime was marginal back then as the Internet was limited to mostly defense setups, large organizations, and research communities. The Internet was launched for public use in 1996 and was instantly popular with the masses to the point that it changed their lives. The Graphical User Interface for the Internet was designed simplistically, making it easier for users to understand the functionalities and characteristics of the Internet. Life was simple, and users only had to click on hyperlinks or type URLs into the browser without having to think about where the data on their browsers came from. They did not need to worry if anyone else had access to the data or if the data they received was snooped or tampered with by an attacker. As the Internet evolved, cybercrime's focus shifted from merely damaging a computer physically or interfering with data to committing financial crimes.

The Internet was at its peak by 2013, and the rate at which cybercrimes were being committed increased rapidly. Twenty-five computers became victims every second, and an estimated 900 million users were already victims of cybercrimes. With almost everyone in the world now owning a smartphone, the number of victims has vastly increased.

Classification of Cybercrimes

Most cybercriminals attack organizations since most organizations maintain a database or server with large volumes of sensitive data about their employees and customers. A cybercriminal can either be an outsider or an employee of the organization. You can classify cybercrimes into two kinds based on this criterion.

Insider Attack

An attack on a system or computer infrastructure by someone who already has access to it is an insider attack. The attacker, in this case, is either an employee or a consultant working in the organization. These attackers perform the hack for various reasons, such as greed and revenge. An insider can perform an attack on the system easily since he or she is aware of the infrastructure, policies, and the weaknesses of the security system. This individual also has access to the organization's network. Therefore, it is relatively easy for an insider to steal information or harm the infrastructure. An insider usually finds a window of opportunity for an attack, especially when they are assigned new roles in the organization. For example, when a company develops a new application, it may not have the necessary controls and policies in place to secure the data in the application. An insider can use this vulnerability to perform the hack. Insider attacks can be detected and prevented by installing intrusion detection systems internally within the organization.

External Attack

External attacks arise when somebody inside or external to the organization hires a hacker to attack the organization's network and systems. External attacks are executed to cause financial and reputational losses to an organization. An external attack needs more planning and research when compared to an insider attack. Every external attack goes through the following stages:

- Planning
- Reconnaissance
- Scanning
- Gaining Access
- Maintaining Access

If the organization's network admin is experienced, he or she constantly checks the firewall logs and scans the systems and network to identify vulnerabilities. The organization can also use intrusion detection systems to detect and prevent external attacks.

In addition to insider attacks and external attacks, there are two more types of cyberattacks: structured or unstructured. This classification is based on the experience of the attacker. Most people classify these attacks as external attacks, but there are cases where an employee has performed structured attacks on the organization for personal gain. These types of attacks are often carried out by rival companies. They may send one of their employees to the company and ask them to collect information from that company. This is known as corporate espionage.

Unstructured Attacks

An attack carried out by an amateur attacker without any predefined motive is classified as an unstructured attack. These attacks are often carried out using a penetration tool readily available on the Internet. The attacker may use this tool on the company's network.

Structured Attacks

A structured attack is planned and executed carefully by an experienced and skilled professional with clear objectives. Attackers have access to powerful tools and technologies that help them access the target system or network without being detected by an intrusion detection system. Additionally, an attacker also has the knowledge required to modify an existing tool to suit the specific attack requirements.

Reasons for Cybercrimes

An attacker can choose to hack a system or network of an organization for multiple reasons. The following are some common reasons why cybercrimes happen.

Money

Attackers commit cybercrimes to earn money since this is an easier and faster way to make money. They use hacking methods, such as phishing and spoofing, to trick someone into revealing their account information. The attacker can use this information to transfer the funds from the victim's account into their own.

Revenge

Some attackers may want to take revenge against another individual, organization, religion, or government. They may choose to hack these entities to cause financial and physical losses. This form of attack is known as cyberterrorism. Some attackers hack systems and networks when they want to test a new tool or software. The only objective of such an attack is to understand how the new tool or software works.

Recognition

Some attackers choose to attack to gain popularity. They may hack a defense or large organization's systems and networks to make a name for themselves—anonymity.

Cybercriminals can ensure their anonymity when they perform a hack. It is extremely easy for cybercriminals to get away with their attack since nobody knows how to trace the attack back to the cybercriminal. This anonymity, at times, has even motivated respectable citizens to commit a cybercrime for personal gain.

Cyber Espionage

Some governments may choose to overlook the data privacy act and track everything their citizens do. They may choose to do this for political or economic reasons.

Types of Cyber Hackers

Hackers are curious about how networks and computer systems work. They are skilled in coding and programming since they do their best to hone their programming skills. They also learn about various tools and technologies they can use to perform hacks. Since hackers attack an operating system, they learn more about the different kinds of systems and find their way around the system to identify any vulnerability.

Here are the most common types of hackers.

White Hat Hackers

Hackers who have certifications and are authorized to conduct penetration tests for an organization or a government to identify vulnerabilities in their information systems are white hat hackers—or also known as ethical hackers or cybersecurity experts. They are a part of the security team in an organization, and their job is to prevent an attack on the organization's system and network. They comply with the rules of engagement stated by the organization or government.

Black Hat Hackers

Black hat hackers, also known as crackers, want to access your system and network and steal, manipulate, or destroy your data. They implement common hacking practices for their attacks. They are lawbreakers or criminals, and it is easy to differentiate between a white hat and black hat hacker based on their objectives.

Gray Hat Hackers

These are hackers that fall in a spectrum between white hat and black hat hackers. Since they are not certified as cybersecurity experts, they can choose to work for or against the organization. The motives of the hacker determine whether he is a white hat or black hat hacker.

Script Kiddies

Script kiddies are known to be the most dangerous people in the hacking world since they lack experience and knowledge. They use any malicious tool or software available on the Internet without learning what it is used for. They also have no idea about the damage they can cause to the network or system. They attack computers and networks intending to mark their presence in the hacking world.

Green Hat Hackers

Green hat hackers are also amateurs of the hacking world, but there is a difference between them and script kiddies. They have little knowledge about hacking and work on developing the necessary skills to hack since they are passionate about becoming professional hackers. They are inspired by other professional hackers and keep in touch with them to learn to hack.

Blue Hat Hackers

Blue hat hackers are script kiddies who have some knowledge about hacking. They are different from green hat hackers since they perform a hack with malicious intentions. However, they do not have the intention to develop the necessary skills to carry out the hack.

Red Hat Hackers

Red hat hackers, also known as eagle eye hackers, are like white hat hackers. They do their best to counter any attacks carried out by black hat hackers. The difference is that red hat hackers are ruthless and destroy the network and systems used by black hat hackers.

State-Sponsored Hackers

As the name suggests, a country or state hires these hackers to hack into other countries' or states' systems to extract defense-related information. They are on the government's payroll.

Hacktivist

The online version of an activist is known as a hacktivist. They are anonymous hackers, and they target government systems for social and political reasons.

Whistleblower

An employee of a government or organization who feels their institution is being unethical and conducting illegal activities may choose to call it out against their conscience. They may also do this for personal gain. Such hackers are known as whistleblowers.

Common Tools Used by Hackers

Hackers use numerous tools to execute the perfect attack. The following are the most common tools in a hacker's toolkit.

Rootkit

A rootkit is an application or a set of tools that allows hackers to gain remote control of a computer or network of computers connected to the Internet. The rootkit was originally developed to open backdoors in any software so that it could be fixed or updated with patches. Hackers tweaked this application to suit their needs. They now use this tool to control the operating system.

Rootkits can be installed in various ways on a target system. The most popular methods are phishing and social engineering. Once rootkits are installed on a target system, the hacker can control that system. They can destroy or steal sensitive information from that system.

Keyloggers

Keyloggers are tools capable of recording every key pressed on the keyboard. Keyloggers cling to the Application-programming Interface of any application and record every keystroke made by the user when they access the application. The recorded keystrokes are saved to a file that contains sensitive data, such as usernames, passwords, website URLs, opened applications, etc.

Keyloggers are scary as they can record credit card details, mobile numbers, personal messages typed in email applications, etc., provided they were typed using the keyboard. Keyloggers are planted using malware such as Trojan horses on a target's computer.

Vulnerability Scanners

As the name suggests, a vulnerability scanner is used to scan networks and computer systems to identify vulnerabilities or gaps. Ethical hackers commonly use this tool to identify loopholes in a system so they can patch them as soon as possible. Black hat hackers also take advantage of vulnerability scanners to discover weaknesses in a target's system or network to exploit them.

Types of Cybercrime

It is also important to understand the crimes a person can commit using digital platforms, such as computers and the Internet. Here are the various types of cybercrimes people commit today.

Cyberstalking

When someone uses the Internet to stalk another person, harass, or threaten them, it is cyberstalking. A cyberstalker often uses applications like email, online messengers, social networking websites, etc., to execute cyberstalking. These mediums offer anonymity. Cyberstalking includes activities such as sexual harassment, monitoring someone's private life, false accusations, etc.

Forgery/Counterfeiting

It is a crime to counterfeit documents. With advanced applications available today, it is easy to create a document that looks exactly like the original. It becomes difficult to differentiate between the correct and fake documents unless you are an expert.

Child Pornography

Possessing, uploading, or downloading the sexual content of a minor is a cybercrime. Multiple websites on the Internet promote child pornography and exploit many minors in the world.

Cyber Terrorism

Some people use digital resources to spread hatred against a religion, country, etc. This is an act of terrorism and is known as cyber terrorism.

Piracy

Content is available digitally today and can be easily copied and distributed over the Internet. Distribution of content owned by someone else is illegal. For example, the illegal distribution of movies or music over the Internet is classified as piracy and is a cybercrime.

Computer Vandalism

Destruction of digital resources, either using physical means or malicious code, is computer vandalism and a cybercrime.

Phishing

Phishing is the process of tricking someone into disclosing their sensitive information, such as bank account details, via email. The attacker sends an email that resembles emails sent from a bank or other financial institutions using a domain similar to the bank's domain. The attacker can ask the victim to provide sensitive information, such as their account number, password, etc. The attacker can then use this information to transfer funds from the victim's account into theirs. If the hacker performs the attack using a telephone, it is known as vishing or voice phishing.

Hacking

Hacking is the act of accessing a computer that does not belong to you to steal, modify, or destroy data present on it. The motive behind performing a hack can be political or social.

Spreading Malware

Some hackers use different websites to spread malware. They may do it for fun or have certain objectives. Malware can destroy systems resulting in financial losses for a business or individual. The losses include the cost of repairing the system and the data destroyed. If the hacker is found, the business can sue them for damages.

Cross-Site Scripting

Some notorious attackers inject a client-side script into the website's code. An innocent user who visits this website ends up executing this script, and the script scans the cookies in the user's network. The script uses the cookies to collect sensitive information and transfer that information to the attacker's system. The attacker can use this information to gain access to the user's computer or sessions on a website and use it to exploit the user financially.

Spamming

The act of sending bulk unwanted and unnecessary emails over the Internet is spamming. An email can be called spam if it is one of the following:

- Anonymous: The sender remains anonymous.
- Bulk Mail: The sender sends one email to multiple users.
- Unsolicited email: The sender did not request the email.

Spam emails not only congest the victim's inbox, but they also congest the network.

Cyber Squatting

The act of registering a domain using a trademark of another organization with the intention of later selling it to the organization that owns it for a high cost is cybersquatting.

Online Auction Frauds

Various websites on the Internet conduct online auctions, and cybercriminals take advantage of these websites. They clone the website, and any payment made during the auction moves to the hacker's account.

Internet Time Thefts

Internet time thefts are mostly a crime of the past where an attacker steals a user's Internet Service Provider (ISP) details and uses that information to surf the Internet at the cost of their time. This means the user is charged for the time spent on the Internet.

Web Jacking

Web jacking is when an attacker hacks an organization's website to display irrelevant information. They may also use this opportunity to spread awareness about the organization's activities. Web jacking serves political, social, or economic interests.

Denial of Service Attack

DoS or Denial of service is where the attacker floods a network with unnecessary traffic so that a website or domain becomes inaccessible.

Email Spoofing

Hackers manipulate headers of an email, so it does not show the source. This is done to trick the recipient into giving away sensitive information.

Salami Attack

A salami attack is marginal in nature and can go unnoticed for a long period. An example of a salami attack is when the attacker targets bank accounts of multiple users to withdraw 1 cent every day from each account. The users would not notice it, but 1 cent from multiple users' bank account over many days can amount to a lot of money in a few months or years. Banks now monitor any unusual withdrawals immediately and notify the owner about the transaction.

Data Diddling

The act of manipulating data before it is entered into a computer system is data diddling. For example, an attacker can change the salary they are due to receive from the company on the day of payroll calculation. They can receive a higher salary from the company, but the company's report shows they were paid the amount they were due.

Logic Bombs

Malicious code injected into genuine software is known as a logic bomb. The malicious code is triggered by an action the user performs. When the malicious code is triggered, it can destroy information on the system or destabilize the system.

Chapter Three: Recognizing and Countering a Phishing Attack

What is Phishing?

Using a phishing attack, an attacker tries to get sensitive information, such as user accounts, bank and credit card details, and other important credentials. As mentioned earlier, the attacker may use electronic media, such as text messages or emails, and pose as a genuine user or organization to trick the end user into clicking a link or downloading an attachment. Since the email looks like it has come from a legitimate source, the user may divulge some sensitive information.

Phishing attacks have been pain points for both individual users and organizations. Any kind of information gained from an individual or organization is valuable as it may help the attacker gain monetary benefits or attack the network used by the organization. Additionally, some states or nations may use phishing attacks to obtain the sensitivity of other countries.

Methods used for Phishing

The most common method used for phishing is an email where the attacker tries to obtain sensitive information by coercing users to access and interact with malicious websites. Here are some other methods that hackers use to perform this attack.

• An attacker may manipulate links in emails sent to you. They do this by changing the URL slightly, so the user cannot differentiate between the malicious link and the actual website. For instance, most web-based applications offer a "Forgot Password" feature. When you click on the button, the website sends you an email to reset the password. If the hacker manages to reroute the email, they can send you a different link where you enter your username and the answer to a security question. The hacker can then use that information to access your account.

- • Some hackers also use website forgery as a means of phishing. This is a process where the attacker uses JavaScript commands to develop a fake website that looks genuine. This makes it easier to track the user.

- • Attackers also make use of a technique known as covert redirection. In this process, they infect genuine websites to throw pop-ups. A user clicks on links in the pop-up that redirect him or her conveniently to the attacker's website.

- • Attackers can deploy malware and ransomware to a user's system or network through infected.EXE attachments, PDFs, and Microsoft Office attachments.

- • Attackers can also perform phishing attacks through other media, such as text messages, telephone calls, and social media.

Common Ways to Tackle Phishing Attacks

This section lists the different methods to protect your system and network from different types of phishing attacks. Some of the common methods used are:

- Malware Scanners
- Auto updates
- Multi-factor Authentication
- System or data backups

This will be detailed later in the book. In addition to the methods mentioned above, there are other techniques you can use to protect your system and network from phishing attacks.

Types of Phishing and How to Protect Yourself against Them

Deceptive Phishing

Deceptive phishing is the most common type of phishing attack. The attacker employs deceptive phishing by imitating a genuine email sender or organization to trick the user into giving out personal information or login details. This is done by using emails. The email content creates a sense of urgency, causing the user to panic and do exactly what the attacker intended them to do.

For instance, the attacker may send an email to one or more users telling them their credit will be deactivated if they do not make the payment using the link in the email body. When the user clicks on the link, they are redirected to the attacker's website, which is a replica of the bank or payment gateway. The user then enters their credit card details, including the expiry date and security code. The attacker now has all the necessary information to make fraudulent transactions on the user's credit card.

The success of a deceptive phishing attack depends on how closely the phishing email resembles that of the actual organization's email. Users need to go through the URLs of both the email address and the links in the email body to protect themselves before they click the link or download any attachments. Other common indications of a deceptive phishing email include spelling and grammar errors, and generic salutations.

Spear Phishing

Not all phishing attacks employ "spray and pray" techniques and are without personalization. Many phishing attacks depend heavily on personalized emails and messages, and this is where spear phishing comes into the picture.

Spear phishing attacks ensure that the name, address, phone number, company, position, job profile, etc., are included in the email body so that the recipient is convinced that they have a relationship with the sender. The objective of spear phishing is ultimately the same as deceptive phishing—to trick the user into clicking on a malicious link or downloading a malicious attachment. The attacker can use either of the two means to obtain sensitive information. Much effort is needed to create a spear phishing email since the attacker must obtain some personal information of the target. Therefore, social websites like LinkedIn are commonplace for spear phishing attackers from where they try to retrieve as much personal information of a target as possible.

The organization must conduct specific training regularly to ensure their users do not respond to such emails. Businesses should also invest in technologies that scan incoming emails for known malware.

Whaling Attack

Spear phishing can be employed to attack everyone in an organization, including top executives, and this is a whaling attack. The attacker targets whales or high-level executives to steal their information and login credentials.

A successful whaling attack can lead to CEO Fraud. As the name suggests, CEO fraud is where the attacker uses the CEO's email to approve large financial transactions once they receive their bank information. Another application of whaling is where attackers use the executive's email account to request other employees' personal information, so they can file fake tax returns using the employees' details. They can also choose to sell this information online.

Most attackers get away with whaling attacks since the top-level management in most organizations is ignorant about information security. Whaling can be avoided simply by making security awareness training mandatory for all employees, including top-level management. Businesses should also implement two-factor authentication or multi-factor authentication processes for financial transactions to ensure they cannot be completed through email alone.

Vishing

The previous phishing attacks depend exclusively on email as a medium for the attack. Email undoubtedly is the most popular phishing medium, but attackers also resort to other media at times.

Vishing is a phishing technique that uses phone calls to scam users. When the telephone gained popularity, people only communicated using it. However, with today's advancement in technology, calls can be made using the Voice over Internet Protocol VoIP, where an attacker can imitate genuine organizations to steal information from a user.

There are various forms of vishing. For instance, in September 2019, attackers launched a vishing attack on the MPs and other parliamentary staff in the United Kingdom to steal their passwords. In the same year, there was another vishing attack where the attackers pretended to be the top management of a German organization and coerced their UK subsidiary to give away information to steal money worth USD 243,000.

The simplest way to avoid vishing is never to answer calls from unknown numbers, use an app for caller identification, and never divulge personal information over the phone to anyone.

Smishing

Vishing is not the only method where attackers use a phone to implement a phishing attack. Attackers also use text messages to perform a hack, and this form of hacking is known as smishing. The message contains a link or a phone number that the receiver must click or call on.

Smishing attackers also pretend to be genuine entities. In February 2019, Nokia sent a warning to everyone in the world where smishers were pretending to be Nokia and sending out messages to users saying they had won money or a vehicle. When the hackers initiated the scam, they would ask users to send them a nominal amount as the registration fee to claim the vehicle they won.

In the same year, there was a story of a woman who was a victim of a smishing attack. The woman had cancer, and the smishers tricked her into believing that they were from the government, offering her a grant to pay for her treatment. The attackers asked her to make a nominal down payment and pay taxes in order to be eligible for the grant.

Again, the simplest way to avoid a smishing attack is to look at the number that is messaging you and then decide to do something about it. Alternatively, it is also a good idea to call the company cited in the message and cross-check if they actually sent any such message.

Pharming

Attackers are aware that users are getting wiser and being trained against common phishing scams. Therefore, most attackers no longer use methods where they need to use bait to obtain sensitive information. They now use pharming, where they take advantage of cache poisoning in the Domain Name System. Domain Name System, or DNS in short, is a naming system used by the Internet to convert strings to IP addresses such as google.com to a numeric IP to land the user on the website for Google.com.

When an attacker employs the DNS cache poisoning technique, they attack a DNS server and change the IP of a certain website to their own IP. This means that the attacker can redirect a user to their website instead of the genuine one. This happens even if the user enters the correct website name.

Pharming attacks can be avoided by training users and employees to enter sensitive information only on websites secured by a digital certificate and resolved on the HTTPS protocol. A business should also install antivirus and anti-malware solutions on all official devices and update virus signatures regularly. Internet Service Providers should also take proactive measures to secure their networks.

Identifying a Phishing Email

This section will go through an example, so you can understand what a phishing email looks like, how to identify it, and what measures can be taken to avoid being tricked by such emails.

What is Email Spoofing?

Email Spoofing is a methodology under the umbrella of Email Phishing where an attacker manipulates the headers of an email to make the source of the email look genuine even when it is coming from an illegitimate source, like the attacker's system. Attackers are aware that users trust an email as long as the sender's email address resembles an address they have seen before. The motive of email spoofing is to trick the user into believing the email they have received is important, and the sender is genuinely requesting information.

Identifying a Spoofed Email

There are two ways to identify a spoofed email:

If the subject line is similar to any of the examples given below, the email is not valid:

- Your email account abc@example.com is hacked
- Urgent: Change your email account's password right away
- Your bank account is hacked
- Security Alert: Save your email accounts

If the email content asks for the following information, it is a spoofed email:

- Personal details or your bank account details
- Requesting you to send money to a particular account
- Password reset link even though you did not request a password change
- Other unknown links to verify details

How do you confirm that the email is indeed a spoofed or spam email from the email headers?

You can determine the authenticity of the email by looking for either of the following parameters within the email source:

Received-SPF

SPF is an implementation of authorization through a TXT DNS record in the domain's DNS zone to authorize emails to be sent only from authorized sources. The syntax contains an IP address added by the domain owner, which means the SPF check in the email headers will pass only if the email originated from that IP. If the email originated from any other IP, the SPF check fails, and the emails are redirected to the spam folder of the recipient.

X-CMAE-Score – 100

This is the spam score of the email. The recipient email server has certain spam checks in place based on what spam score it assigns to the email, 100 being the highest.

This is how the header of an email looks like. You can access the header by viewing the original source of an email in the email provider's interface, like gmail.com.

```
Return-Path: <aishah@pintasan.com>
Delivered-To: aishah@pintasan.com
Received: from mx1.mailhostbox.com ([172.16.214.152])
        by mss-va3.mailhostbox.com with LMTP id KFu1Aa1Q6VsYRAAAgCy1pg
        for <aishah@pintasan.com>; Mon, 12 Nov 2018 19:10:16 +0000
X-Spam-Subject: YES
Authentication-Results: mx1.mailhostbox.com, dkim=none; dkim-atps=neutral
Received-SPF: [Softfail] (domain owner discourages use of this host) identity=mailfrom; client-ip=177.237.3.206; helo=177.237.3.206.rabix-dyn.cableonline.com.mx; envelope-from=aishah@pintasan.com;
receiver=aishah@pintasan.com
Received: from 177.237.3.206.cable.dyn.cableonline.com.mx (unknown) [177.237.3.206])
        by mx1.mailhostbox.com (Postfix) with ESMTP id 9E8A6108910
        for <aishah@pintasan.com>; Mon, 12 Nov 2018 19:10:15 +0000 (GMT)
Message-ID: <680226c2833C4A78E1E57DD07E794BD2@pintasan.com>
From: <aishah@pintasan.com>
To: <aishah@pintasan.com>
Subject: aishah@pintasan.com is compromised. Password must be changed
Date: 12 Nov 2018 03:53:11 -0800
MIME-Version: 1.0
Content-Type: text/plain; charset="ibm852"
Content-Transfer-Encoding: 8bit
X-Mailer: Ypogdsc hpeasd 5.3
X-Spam-Status: Yes
X-CMAE-Score: 100
X-CMAE-Analysis: v=2.3 cv=ovg8PA51 c=8 sm=1 tr=0 p=kYYx:k83HRAqa111iiU6:9
        a=nof5s&f22Vc:FbHyH81P9cXQ+=.117 a=nof5sFT22VcKoHyH8TP9cXQ+=:17
```

The most frequently asked questions when a user receives such an email are:

Is my account compromised if I receive such an email?

No, your email account is not compromised in any way. The email received is either spam or a spoofed email.

Why isn't the server classifying such emails as SPAM?

Most servers have stringent email checks in place that classify these emails as SPAM. These emails automatically move to the Spam folder of the user's email, but there are times when these checks can skip an email.

Can I completely avoid receiving a spoofed email?

No, in every case, the spammer may use a different subject and a different body, so creating a global filter won't help. This filter may block legitimate emails.

Reference Email: (Template Used)

Hi, stranger!

I hacked your device because I sent you this message from your account. If you have already changed your password, my malware will intercept it every time. You may not know me, and you are most likely wondering why you are receiving this email, right?

In fact, I posted a malicious program on adults (pornography) of some websites, and you know that you visited these websites to enjoy (you know what I mean). While you were watching video clips, my Trojan started working as an RDP (remote desktop) with a keylogger that gave me access to your screen as well as a webcam.

Immediately after this, my program gathered all your contacts from messenger, social networks, and also by e-mail. What I've done? I made a double-screen video. The first part shows the video you watched (you have good taste, yes . . . but strange for other normal people and me), and the second part shows the recording of your webcam.

What should you do?

Well, I think $608 (USD dollars) is a fair price for our little secret. You will make a Bitcoin payment (if you don't know, look for "how to buy Bitcoins" on Google).

BTC Address: 1GjZSJnpU4AfTS8vmre6rx7eQgeMUq8VYr (This is CASE sensitive, please copy and paste it)

Remarks: You have two days (48 hours) to pay. (I have a special code, and at the moment, I know that you have read this email). If I don't get Bitcoins, I will send your video to all your contacts, including family members, colleagues, etc.

However, if I am paid, I will immediately destroy the video, and my Trojan will destroy itself.

If you want to get proof, answer, "Yes!" and resend this letter to yourself. And I will definitely send your video to any twelve contacts.

This is a non-negotiable offer, so please do not waste my personal and other people's time by replying to this email. Bye! Please investigate the issue and get back to me.

The attacker has sent this email by spoofing the user's own email address, making them believe they have access to the user's email account. If you look at the content, the attacker is trying to convince an innocent user by saying they have access to the user's computer even when they do not. The user, if not careful, will believe the attacker and give in to their requests. However, examining the headers of the email will help the user understand if this attacker actually has access to their email or is just bluffing.

Most types of phishing scenarios have been covered in this chapter, with an example of email phishing. You can use this as a guide to help you identify and avoid any phishing attacks. This does not guarantee that you can recognize every phishing attempt. Attackers also do their research and learn more about user behavior, and they use this information to improve their attacks. Keeping this in mind, users and organizations should train themselves to learn more about any new phishing techniques hackers use today.

Chapter Four: How to Identify and Remove Malware

Malware is an umbrella term for different malicious software, such as spyware, ransomware, and viruses. Malware is a code developed by attackers to attack a system and associated data or access a third-party network. The medium used to deploy malware is most commonly an email. The email contains links or attachments that, when clicked or downloaded, result in the execution of the malware code.

Malware appeared in the late 1970s, with the introduction of the Creeper virus, which threatened individual users and organizations. Since then, the world has seen thousands of malware variants, all having the same intent—disruption and destruction of services.

The malware contains payloads that are deployed on target systems in various ways. An attacker's motives range from demanding money to stealing information, and they are beginning to get smarter with their attack techniques. Here are the different types of malware present today.

Types of Malware

Some of these terms have already been briefly discussed in the cybersecurity terminology section in Chapter One. In this section, you will understand them in more detail.

Viruses

Virus is a generic term used by regular computer users and the media for any malware that makes the headlines. However, it is unfair to say that all malware is a virus. A computer virus attaches to files on your system or on pointers to those files and gets triggered when the user executes the files. For example, a user may be executing a normal PDF document, and the virus would have leached onto it via embedded code.

The digital domain does not commonly have any pure viruses today as they make up for less than ten percent of malicious software. This is a good thing. The virus is the only subgenre of malware that sits on one file and then spreads to another file. Given this nature, it becomes a difficult task to clean viruses as they can keep spreading. Cleaning up viruses has always been complicated, and even the best antivirus solutions struggle with it. Most antivirus solutions are only capable of detecting and quarantining infected files. They cannot clean them and, therefore, just end up deleting these files as a last resort. One may argue what the harm is in deleting files, but if these files are essential for your application or web application to function, their deletion will lead to malfunction of your application or website.

Worms

The history of the existence of worms predates viruses. They have been present ever since the development of mainframes. They became popular in the 1990s with the introduction of email, and security experts were frustrated with worms arriving as email attachments. One employee would open an email with a worm, and the entire organization would be infected in a short period.

What distinguishes a worm from a virus is that a worm is self-replicating. For instance, the Iloveyou worm, on the days of its inception, took over the world by affecting emails, phone systems, television networks, etc. Other popular worms, like MS Blaster and SQL Slammer, also ensured that they would be remembered forever in computer security history.

A worm is extremely dangerous because it can spread like wildfire without any user interaction. Contrary to this, viruses need a human to trigger them and then infect other files. Worms can just depend on files and processes in the system to execute.

For instance, the SQL Slammer still holds the record to date for exploiting a vulnerability in Microsoft SQL, to create buffer overflows on every SQL server with Internet connectivity within ten minutes.

Trojans

Attackers have moved from worms to Trojans as a weapon for implementing attacks. Trojans pretend to look like genuine programs or files but have malicious code embedded in them. Trojans were present in the digital world even before viruses and are the most popular malware amongst cybercriminals today.

Like viruses, even Trojans need user interaction to be executed. Trojan use emails or malicious websites as a medium to arrive at a target system. The most common and popular type of Trojan is a fake antivirus. You may have seen pop-ups while visiting certain websites that say your computer is infected and asks you to download software to clean the virus. You may believe that it is true and take the bait and end up downloading and installing a Trojan instead. The Trojan then takes control of your system.

It is difficult to defend yourself against a Trojan for two reasons.

1. Trojans are easy to code, and cybercriminal groups have even developed Trojan building kits today.

2. Trojans are deployed onto a system by tricking users, and therefore, they conveniently dodge traditional defenses like a firewall.

There are literally millions of Trojans that are developed every month. Antivirus developers try their best to counter Trojans, but the signatures are too many to keep track of.

Hybrid Malware

The malware present today is a hybrid combination of malicious software, Trojans, and even viruses. The malware may look like a Trojan in the beginning, but its execution will end up attacking all users on the network, a nature exhibited by worms.

Malware programs today are considered to be stealth programs or rootkits. This means that the main objective of malware today is to take control of the computer's operating system and manipulate it in such a way that even anti-malware programs cannot detect it. The only way to get rid of such malware is to disconnect the memory component that has control of the system.

Another hybrid combination of Trojans and worms are bots that exploit one system and try to add it to an attack toward a larger infrastructure. Bots place themselves on individual computer systems and then receive instructions from botmasters, which are command and control servers for the bot network. Bot networks known as botnets can infest a few hundred computers to a network of thousands of servers over the Internet, controlled by a single botmaster. Botmasters often rent these botnets out to other criminals who use them for their specific needs.

Ransomware

Ransomware is malware through which attackers encrypt all your data and demand a ransom to decrypt it. Attackers initially used to target individual users with ransomware but realized the monetary benefits of targeting bigger institutions, such as banks, hospitals, etc. Ransomware will be discussed in depth later.

Fileless Malware

This is not really a different type of malware but has made it as a classification based on the way malware is used to exploit a user.

Traditional malware infects systems by taking control of the file system. On the other hand, fileless malware does not touch the file system but spreads within system memory or employs other non-file components such as APIs, scheduled tasks, and registry keys.

Fileless malware exploits a program running in the system to become its sub-process. Or it uses system tools such as the PowerShell in Microsoft Windows-based operating systems. Attackers have started using fileless malware because they are difficult to detect.

For instance, Operation Cobalt Kitty is a fileless malware that became popular for infecting PowerShells and attacking Asian companies for six months. The malware was deployed onto target systems by using spear phishing emails.

Adware

If you have come across malware only in the form of adware, consider yourself lucky. Adware infects a computer and just keeps popping up unwanted ads. The most common ads that appear through adware redirect users to websites containing promotions for other products. Adware is potentially harmless but can get very annoying.

Malvertising

Do not confuse this with adware, but malvertising makes use of genuine ads to deliver malicious files to a target system. For example, an attacker might pay a website to place a malicious ad on their web page. A user clicking on this ad will be redirected to the attacker's website or will instantly download malware onto the user's system. Often, malware in the ads executes without any user interaction, a technique called drive-by-download.

There have been instances when attackers hacked into big ad engines like Yahoo to deploy malware through their ads into bigger websites, such as Spotify, New York Times, The London Stock Exchange, etc.

Attackers use malvertising to make money. They deploy malware through ads that are capable of crypto mining and ransomware infections.

Spyware

Spyware is a type of malware used by attackers to spy on people's activities. It is mostly used by partners in a relationship to spy on each other, but attackers also use spyware to understand a target's activity and log their keystrokes.

A regular scanner can detect spyware and help you uninstall it.

Virus Vs. Malware

It is a common practice for people today to use malware and viruses interchangeably, but they are not the same. The difference is that malware is the parent term, and a virus can be a kind of malware. In simple terms, a virus can be malware, but all malware is not a virus.

If represented as a Venn diagram, it would look something like this. A virus is a subset of malware, which is a subset of a threat.

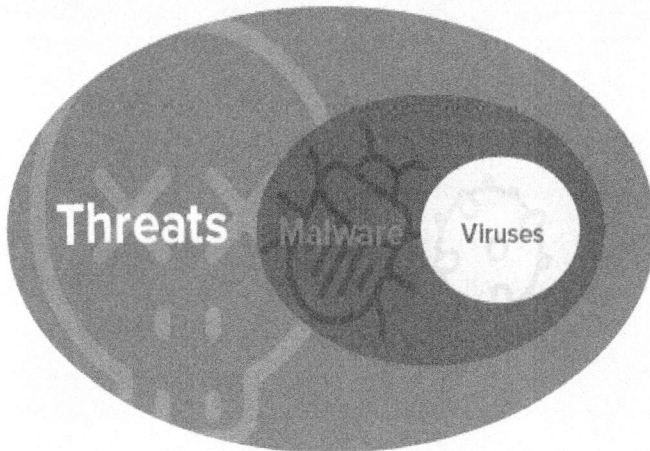

Knowing this, you may now have the following questions.

Why is there confusion if they are different?

Entrenched name recognition is to be blamed for the confusion between a virus and malware. Once a word is put in someone's head, it tends to stay there. For instance, Xerox is a company that deals largely in photocopy machines. However, since the very beginning, a photocopy was known as a xerox, and the term has stuck.

How can you tell if your system has a virus or malware?

A virus will mostly infect one file and replicate itself onto other files. That is the job of a virus if it is purely a virus. However, if the virus was deployed to be malware, the most common indication will be your system slowing down.

Do you need both antivirus and anti-malware?

Today, antivirus and anti-malware solutions are the same thing. No provider will give you a solution that only checks for viruses and leaves out scanning other malware like worms, Trojans, ransomware, etc.

A good security solution will scan local files on the system and also monitor your online activity via email and surfing websites. If you visit a malicious website, your security solution will not even allow it to load in the browser.

Protecting Yourself from Malware

If you feel that your system is infected, follow the steps given below immediately.

Install/Update your Antivirus

If you do not have an antivirus solution, purchase one, and install it immediately. It is a small price to pay for your system's health and the important data it contains. You can trust providers such as Norton Security, Kaspersky, McAfee, and Avast, among many others. Most of these solutions are rated 4.5 stars. Run a deep scan once you have installed the antivirus and let it run even if it takes a lot of time. The only problem is that the malware is very advanced; it knows how to deactivate the antivirus.

If you already have an antivirus solution and it has failed to detect the malware, it mostly means that you have not updated its signatures.

The job is not over by just installing an antivirus solution. New malware is developed every day, and therefore, you need to update your antivirus signatures so that they can detect this new malware. You are opening your system to new malware even if your antivirus is a single day out of the update.

System Restore

Most operating systems, such as Microsoft Windows, have a feature called system restore. This basically stores an image of your entire system at regular intervals. This means that if your system contracted malware today, and there is a system restore point available for yesterday, you could restore your system to how it was yesterday, which will remove the malware. However, sometimes malware code is written so that it won't let you run the system restore. In such cases, you may need to reboot your system to enable safe mode and then try to run a system restore.

Disconnect from the Internet

If there is malware that is being used to steal information from your computer, it means that someone is remotely controlling it through the Internet. The first step to deal with this is disconnecting the Internet completely. Plug out the Ethernet cable, disable Wi-Fi, and even shut down the router if needed.

You may argue that your antivirus will not update if you have disconnected the Internet, but you can install antivirus through an offline solution. At least you will be at peace that the attacker no longer has access to your information.

Get a Portable Antivirus Solution

If everything is failing, and you are not even allowed to install antivirus, it means the malware has taken control of the operating system. You need to find a way to take control without having to deal with the operating system.

In such cases, you can use portable antivirus solutions that can be loaded on to a USB drive. Some of these are ClamWin, Kaspersky

Security Scan, McAfee Stinger, and Microsoft Safety Scanner. You can, in fact, have all of these on a USB drive and run individual scans without causing any conflict.

The aftermath of a malware infection can be difficult at the beginning. It is like coming back to live in a home that was robbed. It will take time to feel safe again. Once you are back, take steps to increase the security of your system. Get the best security solutions, even if they cost a bit. Also, uninstall unwanted software at regular intervals, and delete temporary files. You can be ruthless and strict, but also careful at the same time.

Chapter Five: Recovering from Ransomware

In recent years, you may have heard of the term Ransomware in your office or on the news. What is the fuss all about? Perhaps you received a pop-up on your computer screen saying your system is infected by ransomware. This chapter sheds light on what ransomware is, its types, a little history, and what you should do to protect your systems.

Defining Ransomware

Ransomware is the conjunction of the words ransom and malware. It is malware that infects your computer and encrypts all the data on it, restricting you from accessing it. It then demands a ransom payment if you wish to access all the data again. Ransomware first featured in the 1980s and payments were demanded via snail mail. Today, ransomware is much more evolved, and hackers demand payments via credit cards or cryptocurrency.

How Can You Get Infected?

Attackers can use ransomware in different ways to infect your system. A common way to do this is to fill your inbox or desktop with malicious spam, also known as malspam, where the medium used to deliver spam is an email. The email contains malicious attachments, such as word documents or PDF files, or even hyperlinks to third party websites.

The malspam method employs social engineering tactics to make people believe the email and its attachments are genuine. The hacker does this by making them appear as if they come from a trusted source. Attackers also use social engineering in ransomware attacks where they pose to be the FBI to scare users and make them pay to access their files.

Malvertising is another popular ransomware infection method that peaked around 2016. As the name suggests, malvertising employs the method of online advertising to spread ransomware. This type of ransomware did not interact too much with the users. Even today, you may come across websites filled with ads that redirect you to third-party websites without your permission. These third-party websites are kept to log all your activities and information. They then deploy malware on your computer. Most often, this malware turns out to be ransomware. Malvertising makes use of a technology called iframe that has malware hidden in invisible HTML elements. This iframe will redirect you to a malicious website, and the malware will be conveniently deployed to your computer from this website through an exploit kit. This process is called a drive-by-download process as everything happens without the user knowing what is happening.

Types of Ransomware

Ransomware is classified into three types based on their severity.

Scareware

Scareware is ransomware used to carry out tech support scams on old security software. You may receive pop-ups on your device asking you to download some information from a website. The pop-up may say there is a virus on your system, so you do exactly what the pop-up says, and find that your system is infected with a virus. If you ignore the message, several other pop-ups follow. However, your files will still be safe.

If you have an anti-malware solution from a genuine provider, run it and see if there is some virus on your system. If you do not have an anti-malware solution on your computer, download one immediately before you resort to downloading anything from the link they share with you.

In this case, the attacker is bluffing and trying to scare you in the hopes you fall for the trap.

Screen Lockers

This type of ransomware is an orange-level or medium type of ransomware. As the name suggests, this form of ransomware locks the target user out of their system. When the user tries to unlock the system, they can only see the US Department of Justice's logo or the FBI's logo. The message on the screen may say that they were caught doing something illegal, and therefore, must pay a fine.

Firstly, it is important to know that any law institution will not lock you out of your computer or ask for a payment. If the FBI suspects you, they will contact you directly via legal channels.

If you find yourself in a situation where your screen is locked and you cannot enter the system without making a payment, your system has been hacked.

Encryption Ransomware

This is the most dangerous form of ransomware because an attacker deploys encryption ransomware onto the victim's system and encrypts all the files so the victim cannot access them. They then demand a payment to decrypt all the files to the original state again. It is considered the most threatening form of ransomware due to how difficult it is to decrypt files once encrypted—since no software can decrypt all forms of encryption. It is best to assume those files are lost unless you want to pay the ransom. There is no guarantee that you will get your files even after payment.

Ransomware History

The first occurrence of ransomware was in the 1980s, and it was called AIDS or PC Cyborg. This ransomware encrypted all files of a user present in the C: directory every time the user restarted the system. The ransomware collected all the files after 90 such reboots and then would send the user an email asking them to renew the license to the operating system. They may ask them to pay $189 to PC Cyborg Corporation. It was a very simple encryption technology, and therefore, was easy to reverse. Thus, users from the computer science industry knew how to reverse it, but it majorly impacted common people who were not so tech savvy.

Over the next ten years, a few other variants appeared, but dangerous ransomware did not make a debut until 2004. This was the year when GpCode took advantage of weak RSA encryption to encrypt user files.

The next big ransomware showed up in 2007 when WinLock was introduced. Unlike other ransomware, WinLock did not encrypt user files but locked a user out of their system. It also showed pornographic images on the user screen. The attackers would then demand payment via SMS to grant the users access to their systems.

Ransomware evolved in 2012 with the development of the ransom family called Reveton. This gave birth to another type of ransomware known as law enforcement ransomware. Attackers locked people out of their systems and left the FBI's official logo or any other law enforcement agency's on the lock screen. There would be a statement saying you committed a crime, such as downloading pirated content, hacking, or watching pornographic content on the screen. They would also imply to the target that they must pay a fine ranging from $100 to $3,000 using a prepaid cash card.

Some people did not understand this, and they believed they had broken the law, and therefore, had to pay a fine. This is a social engineering tactic called "implied guilt," where a user questions his or her actions. They don't want to be called out publicly for an activity like watching porn, which they believe is a crime, and so prefer paying the ransom to end it immediately.

Encryption ransomware resurfaced in 2013 with CryptoLocker but was far more dangerous. The CryptoLocker ransomware employed military level encryption, and the hacker would store the decryption key on a remote server. There was no way for users to retrieve their files without paying a ransom. This type of ransomware is even present today, and some cyberattackers are still making money off it. The recent ransomware outbreaks such as Petya and WannaCry in 2017 also made use of similar encryption techniques.

As 2018 came to an end, another ransomware called Ryuk was developed by skilled hackers, and this created trouble for news publications in America, especially the Onslow Water and Sewer Authority in North Carolina. This ransomware attack was planned, so the attackers could first infect the target systems using information-stealing Trojans called TrickBot and Emotet. They would then use this information to install Ryuk and other ransomware in the system. Cybersecurity experts believe that hackers used TrickBot and Emotet to target high-profile business people. These Trojans infected random systems and deployed Ryuk once they identified that the target system belonged to a high-profile businessman, and the attacker could make a lot of money.

Coming to the present day, a new type of ransomware called Sodinokibi, known to be an evolution of GandCrab, has been making news. The attackers use managed service providers to spread this ransomware. In August 2019, several dental care centers lost large volumes of data, and hospitals were unable to obtain records of their patients. The attackers used a compromised manager service provider to upstream the ransomware to 400 dental care centers.

Who are Targets of a Ransomware Attack?

When ransomware was invented, the primary victims of it were individuals who were regular computer users. Attackers realized later that ransomware had more potential, especially when they began to target businesses. When an attacker used ransomware to attack a business, they ensured they could stop the production, and create a loss in data and revenue. Attackers soon realized that attacking a business would fetch more money than attacking regular users. At the end of 2016, statistics showed that ransomware was detected on roughly thirteen percent of global businesses and only two percent of regular users' computers. By 2017, almost 35 percent of small and medium-sized businesses were already victims of ransomware.

Geographically speaking, attackers deploy ransomware mostly on western markets, and the United Kingdom, the United States, and Canada are their biggest targets. Research shows that ransomware attackers always choose businesses and countries with more money. This means they look for regions where computer and Internet adoption rates are high, and the region is wealthy. It is believed that they will target the Asian and South American markets very soon, too, as these regions are picking up in terms of economic growth.

What to Do If You Are Infected

The thumb rule to follow if you are a victim of ransomware is never to pay the ransom. Even the FBI encourages you not to pay. If you pay the ransom, you end up doing what the attacker wants you to do. Therefore, you may encourage them to continue plotting ransomware attacks for the future. There is a small probability that you may get some of your files back using free file decryption software.

However, there are only some ransomware attacks that these tools can reverse or prevent. Also, if a decryptor is available, you must ensure it helps to protect the system from ransomware already present on your system. It is advisable not to run any decryption software without knowledge as you may just end up encrypting your files even more. It is also important to look closely at the ransom message that appears or seek help from an IT security consultant.

Other known methods for cleaning ransomware include anti-ransomware products to scan your system and remove the infection. These solutions may not help you retrieve your files but clean your system. In cases of a screen locker, try to restore the system to a previous health point or try running a scan from a bootable USB drive or DVD.

If you want to defeat a ransomware attack while it is in progress, you must stay alert at all times. If you notice slowness in your system for no reason, it is best to restart the system and disconnect the Internet. This ensures that the malware is inactive when you boot the system. It also cannot send or receive instructions from the commanding server or attacker. This means that since the attacker has not completed the activity, they cannot have encrypted all files in the system, and thus, cannot demand money. At this point, you must install an anti-malware solution and run a complete scan of your system.

How Do You Protect Yourself from Ransomware?

Most security experts worldwide have one thing to say when it comes to protecting your system from ransomware—they ask you to prevent the attack from happening.

There are a few methods to tackle a ransomware infection, but there is no evidence that they work. Most of them also require high-level technical expertise, and an average user may not be ready for such tools. Therefore, it is suggested that you follow the remedies below.

The first step is to purchase a paid anti-malware solution that provides real-time protection. This solution can also detect attacks from advanced ransomware. The solution should also be capable of protecting vulnerable files and software while also blocking ransomware from encrypting any files. One such solution is the paid version of Malwarebytes, which protected users from all types of major ransomware attacks in 2017.

The next step takes time and effort. You must regularly create backups of your data and store it on external media. Experts recommend that you store backups on a cloud-based solution that is protected via encryption and multiple-factor authorization. Another option is to store the backups on external media like USB drives or hard disks. However, ensure you disconnect them after you take the backup. Otherwise, there is high chance ransomware may infect these external devices too.

The next step is to ensure your operating system and other software is up to date. The popular WannaCry ransomware exploited a vulnerability in the Microsoft operating system. Microsoft released an update in March 2017 to patch the vulnerability, but most people ignored this update and did not download it. This left their systems open to an attack. It is understood that manually updating the operating system and other software is difficult, and therefore, it is best to enable automatic updates for the operating system and other software.

Finally, it is best to stay informed. The most common technique used by an attacker to deploy ransomware is social engineering. Educate yourself and your employees about how to detect malicious websites, malspam, and other harmful media. Always trust your instincts. If something seems harmful, it probably is.

How Does Ransomware Affect a Business?

Many businesses have been hit hard in the past few years by different types of ransomware, such as WannaCry, SamSam, GandCrab, and NotPetya. The number of ransomware attacks on businesses increased by 88 percent in the second half of 2018 as attackers stopped attacks on computers and normal users' systems. Attackers understood that they could earn more when they attack big businesses, such as government agencies, hospitals, and other commercial institutions. The average damage done by ransomware, including data loss, reparations, fines, and ransom payments, comes to about $4 million.

The latest ransomware attacks were identified as GandCrab attacks. GandCrab made its first appearance in January 2018 and has since been evolving to make the encryption stronger, empowering attackers to attack high-profile organizations. Reports suggest that GandCrab has managed to cause damages worth $300 million in ransoms, most of which have already been paid. The range of individual ransoms is between $600 and $700,000.

In March 2018, another ransomware attack was initiated using SamSam ransomware. This attack was launched on the city servers in Atlanta, which infected essential city services, such as police record systems, and revenue collection systems were infected. SamSam caused $2.6 million in damages to Atlanta.

Chapter Six: How to Spot and Stop a Social Engineering Attack

Social Engineering is the process of manipulating or tricking people into giving you the information you need about them. Cybercriminals are looking for all kinds of information, but most commonly, they employ social engineering to coax you into disclosing your bank information, login credentials to various applications, or passwords to access your computer. They may use this information to transfer funds from your accounts to theirs or install malware on your system.

Cybercriminals use social engineering because they know it is easier to win a person's trust than hack software. For instance, they can use simple conversations to manipulate any victim to give you their password. They do not try to hack the system using a password or any other technical process. They may attack the system if the user has a weak password.

The basic principle of security is to know who and what to trust. You must know when to trust a person and be alert when you communicate with them, especially online, since you cannot see them. This holds true for trusting applications too. You must know whether an application you download and install on your system or website is genuine and won't harm you.

Any security professional will tell businesses that the weakest point in a security chain is a user who accepts and trusts another user at face value. In simple words, it does not matter if you have top-notch security for your house with multiple locks, guard dogs, floodlights, alarm systems, barbed wire, fences, etc., if you let a stranger enter your home simply because they claim to be a plumber without doing any checks. In a case like this, you empowered the threat to enter your house.

Social Engineering Methodologies

There are three types of methodologies employed for social engineering:

- Phishing

- Vishing

- Impersonation

Phishing and Vishing were discussed in Chapter Three; however, Impersonation is when an attacker pretends to be someone you already know and tricks you into giving them access to your computer, network, etc. An attacker does a lot of research before using the impersonation technique to hack your accounts and systems. Attackers stalk people on social media and company websites and gather information about the victim's friends and colleagues. They may also eavesdrop on your conversations and try to sniff around documents you have trashed.

Here are a few statistics to help you understand these social engineering methods concerning their application in the real world.

Phishing

- Seventy-seven percent of the social engineering attacks carried are implemented through phishing.

- Roughly 40 million people report phishing attacks every year.

- Eighty-eight percent of all reported phishing was via links clicked within emails.
- Ninety percent of all email traffic in the world is full of spam and viruses.

Vishing

- Sixty percent of adults in the USA were victims of vishing in 2012.
- 2.4 million customers were targets of phone fraud in the year 2012.
- 2.3 million customers were targets of phone fraud in the first half of 2013 itself.
- USD 42,500 was the average loss per customer to a business.
- When a vishing SMS was received, 60 percent of users clicked on the link in the message, twenty-six percent of users tried to call the number, and fourteen percent of users replied to the text.

Impersonation

- 1.8 million people were victims of impersonation in the USA in 2013. Medical identity thefts increased because of websites impersonating medical providers.
- Eighty percent of thefts happened at the workplace that involved bypassing controls.
- Eighty-eight percent of the stolen information was personal data.
- The average age of a victim of impersonation was 42 years, and the average loss incurred by them was USD 4,200.

Spotting a Social Engineering Attack

What does a social engineering attack usually look like? The following are some common scenarios to understand how social engineering works.

An Email from a Friend

If the attacker manages to hack a user's email password via software or social engineering, the attacker has access to that user's contact list. Given that most users use the same password for numerous web applications, the attacker may gain access to the user's social media and contacts on social media too.

From here on, everything is home territory for the attacker. They can send emails to the user's contacts or instant messages on social media. Most of the messages sent by the attacker have the following features:

- A URL, where the attacker pretends to be a friend and excites you by saying something you can relate to. They may send you a link and ask you to provide some information through that link. Unsuspecting and innocent, because it came from a friend, you click on the link and download malware that infects your computer. The attacker can access your system and perform any action they want. They try to collect information about your contacts and deceive them as they deceived you.

- An image, a video, or music file with a malicious code embedded in the file. You may download the file without hesitation since it's coming from a friend and end up infecting your system with malware. The attacker has access to your computer and the treasure of information that is present on it.

An Email from a Trusted Source

Social engineering is a parent of phishing attacks where attackers imitate a trusted source to trick users into disclosing sensitive information. Reports from Webroot suggest that most attackers impersonate financial institutions. Data from Verizon also suggests that 93 percent of breaches happening today are a result of a successful social engineering attempt.

Emails from trusted sources may have the following themes:

The emails may ask for urgent help

Some emails may have urgent messages, and the sense of urgency may force you into performing the action in the email. Since you are afraid, you may transfer the funds into the attacker's account.

The email may ask for donations for a cause

The emails may try to exploit your generosity or kindness. The content may say that you need to transfer some funds toward a foundation or cause, but the money goes directly into the attacker's account.

Phishing attempts using a genuine background

An attacker may send you a message or email asking you to send funds. The source of the message or email appears to be from a reputed company, school, or institution.

The email will say there is a problem and ask you to click on a link to rectify it

The URL used to send the email may look genuine, and the body of the email may also use a logo similar to the organization the attacker pretends to be from. It's possible that the attacker sent the email directly from the source website, but uses different means to gain access to that website. Since everything looks legitimate, you may click on the URL, which redirects you to the attacker's website. The attacker may present a form that asks for some information they need to hack into your account. The email also includes a warning that tells you what the consequences might be if you do not click on the URL. This may scare you, and you choose to click the link.

Pretend to be your manager or colleague

The email may have details of a project that you were working on at your office. This will gain your trust. The next part will be related to some kind of payment using a company card you have made in the past. You believe this is legitimate and make the payment.

Tell you that you have won something

You may have received emails from a supposed dead relative, a lottery company, or any other business. Some emails may also say you were the 100th person to have visited the website, and you won something. The email asks you to provide some sensitive documents, such as your social security number, to prove who you are. These requests should make you suspicious. Do not trust the emails. This type of attack is known as greed phishing. Since you are greedy, you may want to give the attacker the necessary information. As a result, you may provide sensitive information that the attacker can use to empty your bank account.

Baiting

In this social engineering scenario, the attackers know they can bait the user, especially if they want to obtain sensitive information. Such baits are often found on websites offering free movies or music downloads. Attackers may run such scams on malicious websites, social media, and other websites most users stumble upon via search results.

The baiting scheme also shows up on a website that offers to sell an iPhone for only $100 when the actual cost is $1,000. You may be suspicious, but you see that many users have testified that the offer is true. The attacker obviously planned this.

Users who fall for this bait download malware to their computers and this exposes their details and other sensitive information about other users the victim corresponds with. You may even pay them $100 but never receive the promised iPhone in return.

Responding to Questions that You Didn't Ask

At times, attackers may contact you to provide help from a company, while offering benefits. The email ID may resemble one of a renowned company or bank. If you are not a consumer of the product, you will discard the email. However, there is a high chance that you do use the product and were actually planning to contact the company for help. How convenient that the company approached you proactively to extend their help.

For instance, you may not have asked for help regarding an issue with your operating system, but you suddenly see an email from Microsoft. The email offers to fix the issue for free. You respond to them and trust them, opening yourself up to several exploits the attacker has already planned.

The attacker may ask you to validate yourself and ask you to provide the required information to log into the system or application. Other times, they may ask you to run a few commands on your system to fix the issue. When you let them do this, they access your system.

Distrust Creation

Certain social engineering practices are only implemented to create distrust or conflicts. These are executed by people you know and have a problem with or by people who just enjoy watching the world burn. These attackers will fill your head with wrong impressions of other people you know and then enter as a savior to gain your trust. Such ill practices are also employed by extortionists who want to manipulate you initially and attack you later.

This type of social engineering is initiated by gaining access to one of your accounts. This is achieved by hacking your password, social engineering, or just guessing your password.

The attacker who now has access to your media, like videos and images, may edit them as per their needs and forward it to your contacts to create distrust. They pretend as if the content was forwarded by mistake. The attacker may also use the stolen media content to blackmail the user they hacked or the person they were forwarding the content to.

Social engineering attacks have many variations. The attacker's imagination is the only limit to the number of ways they can exploit someone. A single attack may contain multiple numbers of exploits.

The attacker may then sell your information to people who dislike you so you can be exploited further.

How to Avoid Falling for Social Engineering

The shelf life of a social engineering attack is short, and it needs only a few users to fall for it to be successful. However, you can protect yourself against it. It does not even need too much effort as you just need to be aware of your surroundings most of the time.

Tips

Take it Slow

It is a good idea to slow down and give it some thought. Attackers expect you to act urgently without thinking. Most social engineering attacks put you in a situation that looks urgent. This should be your clue to slow down and review the situation properly.

Spend Some Time on Research

Even if you receive an email from a business you believe you know, go through it thoroughly, not just the body of the email but also the "from" address, the signature, etc. In case you do not recognize the company, do a simple search to see if they really exist.

Don't Blindly Click on Links

If you receive a link in an email, do not click the link. Make some manual effort to find that website URL through a search and see where the base URL leads you. This way, you are in control of the link and not vice versa.

Be Aware of Email Hacking

Attackers hack email accounts and prey on the contacts of the hacked account based on their trust. Therefore, when you receive an email from someone you know, ask yourself if you were expecting it. Do not click on any link in the mail if you did not expect the mail. It would be a good idea to call the person up and verify if they actually sent you the mail.

Do Not Blindly Download

If you do not know the sender, do not download any attachments in the email.

Know that Lotteries are Fake

No one gives you a whole lot of money for free. So, if you receive an email saying you won something, especially without participating in any kind of competition, it is a scam. A classic example is a scene from *Harry Potter and the Order of the Phoenix*, where Tonks sends a letter to the Dursleys saying they won a competition for the best lawn. She only did this so that the Dursleys did not get in the way when they tried to take Harry to the Burrow. If you receive such an email, it is fake.

Look out for Banking Scams

If the email asks for personal and banking information, it is most likely a scam. Delete this email, also create a filter to discard all future emails from that sender.

Reject Offers for Help

Genuine companies do not proactively contact you and ask you to extend any kind of help. If you receive communication from anyone, especially when you do not initiate the conversation, it may be a scam if they say they can do the following:

1. Offer to help you improve your credit score

2. Fix an application or software on your system

If you receive an email or message from a charity that you do not know, delete it. If you really want to donate to a charity, do some research and donate to a legitimate charity.

Configure Your Spam Filters

Spam filters are a feature to help you classify emails as legitimate or spam. Take some time and play with your spam filters. Set rules to allow only emails you want. There are guides available via your email provider on how to set your spam filters. An investment of time, as low as thirty minutes, will make your "email life" easy forever.

Secure All Your Devices

Install antivirus and anti-malware programs on all your devices, and set the software to run a routine scan. The software must run real-time scans for any incoming email. Ensure that you keep your operating system and other software up to date by enabling automatic updates.

Chapter Seven: Network Security and Protection Techniques

This chapter defines network security and the various processes associated with it. It also looks at the different types of cyberattacks that can affect your business and sheds light on how important it is to secure your network if you want to prevent a catastrophic loss.

Network Security

Network security is an umbrella term covering a variety of processes, technologies, and devices. Network security is the configuration of rules and policies in both hardware and software of any web application or tool to secure the integrity, accessibility, and confidentiality of computer data. This is closely associated with network infrastructure.

Computer data and networks are vulnerable to numerous cyberattacks, and some of these were looked at earlier in the book. Therefore, every business, irrespective of its size, infrastructure, or industry, needs to have network security measures in place.

The network architecture is evolving and becoming more complex every day. The threat environment is also constantly changing with attackers trying to find newer methods to exploit security vulnerabilities in the system. Vulnerabilities exist in various assets of network infrastructure such as data, devices, applications, and users. Given this, there are individual tools available to secure these assets. You can also use these tools to test the applications to ensure the business meets with the regular compliance terms. Network security is of the utmost importance as even a few minutes of downtime can damage the organization's reputation and finances.

How Does the Network Security Function?

Network security across an organization has multiple layers. An attacker can target any layer in the network security model. Therefore, businesses need to define network security models for both hardware and software to tackle the vulnerable areas.

There are three aspects to network security: physical, technical, and administrative.

Physical Network Security

This aspect deals with different types of physical access to network-related devices such as cables, modems, switches, and routers. An organization must ensure only authorized employees, especially those who are a part of the IT or network team, have access to these components. Some common ways in which the business can authorize access is through biometrics, security locks, etc.

Technical Network Security

This aspect deals with the protection of data stored on a network or in transit via the network. The business must include twofold protection to protect data and its associated systems from unauthorized access. Care should also be taken to protect data against malicious activities from internal employees. Internal employees may not do it intentionally, but actions such as using a personal USB drive on company property can be a threat.

Administrative Network Security

This aspect deals with processes and security policies to keep user behavior in control. This includes the authentication of users and the level of access based on the role and designation of the user in the organization. For example, a management bank user does not need technical access to a server or network device.

Top Five Attacks Through a Network that can Affect Your Business

The previous chapter briefly discussed the different types of cyberattacks. This section discusses the top five cyberattacks through a network that can destroy your business.

From scheduling recruitments to customer relationship management, most organizations perform all their tasks online. Automation has reduced human effort and made processes much more efficient and convenient, opening up a window of opportunities for cyberattackers.

A report released by the Center of Strategic and International Studies states that the damage caused by cyberattacks is $600 billion annually. The evolution of technology has led to the development of new methods for attackers to scam a business. Here are the top five cyberattacks that businesses have to deal with.

Advanced Persistent Threat (APT)

This attack's objective is to scan the organization's network and software for vulnerabilities and use those vulnerabilities to steal data. An advanced persistent threat can go undetected for a long period. This attack was first introduced by attackers who wanted to steal government information. Attackers now use this method to steal sensitive information from organizations and claim ransom.

Some indicators to help you determine whether your organization is a victim of an advanced persistent threat are as follows:

- Irregular flow of information – You may notice that the infrastructure is witnessing a sudden increase in inbound or outbound traffic. The flow of data has an irregular pattern, and this can happen between networks, servers, or server to client connections.

- Data bundle usage – An advanced persistent threat collates stolen data before transferring it to the desired computer. If you observe huge volumes of data or compressed data being transferred through your network, it indicates that your network may be infected.

- Increased number of user logins during unexpected hours.

- When you discover backdoor Trojans on the network and associated devices.

Denial of Service Attack (DoS)

A denial of service attack is an attack to prevent access to a genuine user from services, such as bank accounts or email accounts. An attacker attacks the network and server and floods the bandwidth with unnecessary requests. The motive of a Denial of Service attack is not to steal any information but to prevent access to the server or website. The business may incur huge financial losses due to this business.

Assume that a user is trying to access their online bank account. They are unable to do so, despite having good internet connectivity. This indicates that the service is under a DoS attack, and genuine users are blocked from accessing their accounts.

Internet of Things (IoT) Hacking

Internet of Things refers to the devices connected to the Internet either directly or indirectly. When business setup is mentioned, it includes various IoT devices such as thermostats, locks, cameras, etc. An attacker can leverage IoT devices to attack a business. For instance, there are several IoT devices that businesses forget to update with the security and contain many vulnerabilities. Say an employee connects their smartwatch to a computer at work. If the smartwatch has vulnerabilities, the attacker can exploit those to access the entire infrastructure at work.

It would make sense to uninstall applications on old and unused IoT devices to ensure an attacker cannot take advantage of them.

Structured Query Language (SQL) Injection

Structured Query Language (SQL) Injection is a hacking method discovered years ago but is still effective today. SQL is a language operated on databases and tables programmed in Oracle, MySQL, or Microsoft SQL. The injection affects any application that uses one of these databases, but attackers target websites that employ these databases. Many cases of SQL injection attacks have happened in the past decade.

If an SQL injection attack is successful, the attacker can modify a website's content and retrieve sensitive information, such as user account details. There are two stages to an SQL injection. In the first stage, the attacker observes the target infrastructure and gathers as much knowledge about it as possible. This stage is also known as Reconnaissance. The next stage is the attack stage, where the attacker uses the information collected to break into the target system. In an SQL injection attack, the attacker embeds malicious code in an SQL command to execute their commands.

Man in the Middle

A man in the middle attack is when a third party intercepts the communication between two parties. There are various online channels the attacker can hack to intercept the data, such as websites, social media, emails, messengers, etc. An attacker employing this attack can access your personal and business transactions. A man in the middle attack can stop a message from reaching you or redirect it to someone else.

This is why most communication applications use end-to-end encryption. This means that when you send a message, an algorithm converts plain text into encrypted characters. Once the recipient receives this script, the algorithm on their device decrypts the characters into plain texts again. This way, the information, even if intercepted by someone in the middle, is useless since they do not know how to decrypt it.

These are some of the common attacks businesses fall prey to. The next section looks at different methods you can use to protect your business.

Protecting your Business from a Cyber Attack

Multiple businesses are hit by cyberattacks regularly. Most attackers target those businesses with outdated security features. Here are the various ways through which you can avoid cyberattacks. You can classify these methods into the following types:

- Cybersecurity through hardware
- Cybersecurity through configurations and settings

Cybersecurity through hardware

Security Keys

You may have heard a friend or team member say they have the same password for all their accounts. They may also say their password is their birth year or other simple words. Therefore, without a doubt, the biggest vulnerability in the cybersecurity domain is people.

The tool Yubikeys allows employees to access their accounts without using a password. They also do not have to manage the number of passwords they need to change. Such applications gain a lot of popularity since attackers can use brute force attacks to hack this software. They may use a different combination of letters, numbers, and characters until they find the right password. Businesses should purchase a key for all employees or team members working on sensitive projects. When they do this, they can plug the key into a device and access the required tools, applications, documents, etc.

Many times, an attacker can also trick an employee through phishing to obtain sensitive information. Attacks that lead to maximum damage are results of traps set through social engineering that bypass security flags, and those that do not set off any alarms.

An experienced attacker tries to learn about an employee and get to know intricate details about them. They may obtain information about the people they communicate with regularly. The attacker then disguises themselves as someone the victim knows and sends you an email from an ID similar to the acquaintance's email. The attacker can use these emails to coax you into clicking malicious links to obtain information about the victim.

Yubikeys can help avoid such scenarios and provide additional security features, such as identifying malicious files or links.

VPN Firewalls

You protect your house from thieves by locking the doors and windows. This also helps you safeguard the people at home. You must maintain these locks on your system and network to prevent unauthorized access to your system and network. Senior leadership teams find it surprising when security teams advise them regarding a physical piece of security equipment. Most retaliate with questions like, "Doesn't my computer's built-in firewall protect me?" Yes, but it does not guarantee the security demands of a business.

All communication irrespective of the location can be encrypted using a VPN Firewall. You may be seated in your office or coffee shop and still maintain a secure connection with the Internet. A firewall can maintain secure communication lines with anybody you want to speak with. This helps tackle Remote Desktop brute force attacks, which is the most common type of ransomware attack. A

VPN firewall also monitors and logs break-in attempts and provides features to filter employees' access, so they do not access harmful websites.

You can save costs by purchasing a refurbished firewall. However, after the purchase, ensure it is updated with the latest firmware before adding employees to the security policies. Make sure to change the default password of the firewall and configure two-factor authentication for admin access. Nowadays, many firewalls also have a software component for employees to install on their official devices. This process may increase the login process time by a few seconds but ensure better security.

Cybersecurity through Configurations and Settings

Multi-factor Authentication

Most applications offer two-factor authentication, but users are very reluctant to use it. However, this security setting is very effective and much needed today. Here is how it works. The user first logs in to their application using their username and password. After this, the system or application triggers a one-time temporary password, which is sent to another device connected to the application and user, like their smartphone. The user can only access the application once they enter this password.

This cuts out the risks from the probability of an attacker having acquired the user's username and password via methods such as email phishing, malware, or keyloggers. This means the attacker enters your username and password but does not receive the one-time password. This blocks the attacker from the application. The application may send a notification to the user if the attacker tries to hack the application multiple times.

Password Vault

Since users access multiple applications, they must maintain different passwords, but most users use the same password across all applications and devices. They do this so that they do not forget the password. There are password vault applications available today that allow users to store their passwords. That way, you must remember one password for the vault. The password vault has features to create complex passwords, manage, and auto-fill passwords into forms, applications, websites, and system logins. These passwords are random and complex and, therefore, difficult for an attacker to crack.

Auto Updates

As mentioned earlier, most businesses do not update their software and applications, which makes the system and network vulnerable and prone to attacks. Software providers regularly provide patch and software updates to maintain the security of the applications. Whenever a new vulnerability is discovered in the software, vendors create a patch for it to secure the application or software. Therefore, if you do not update the software regularly, you leave the software and application open to any incoming attack. Thus, it is wise to leave all your software on auto-update, so it automatically downloads any patch developed by the vendor to cover the vulnerability.

Full Disk Encryption

Every device part of a business must always be fully encrypted. This means that devices such as mobiles, laptops, hard drives, and network storage must always have an encryption layer. Since most businesses allow employees to work from home, they need to ensure any business devices and data are encrypted. For a low cost, full disk encryption ensures that your data is secure if it is ever stolen.

Malware Scanners

Malware scanners are available at low costs and help to detect any malware threats. The market offers different types of malware scanners, and these are classified based on their functionality and price. As discussed previously, it is important to regularly update your malware scanner to ensure that it detects new vulnerabilities.

IP Address Lockdown

Whenever you work on online applications, it is important to lock the IP addresses down, especially those that access the application. Additionally, you can add two-factor authentication to the application to determine if the user is accessing it. It is better to use a multi-factor authentication before you give the users access to the system.

If you use third-party applications for business purposes, it makes sense to lock the IP addresses that have access to the applications down too. This helps prevent logins from unauthorized IPs, and these IPs belong to attackers from other countries or regions.

System Backups

If you grow crops but do not build a fence around the farm, you allow people to tread on the crops or allow rodents to enter and damage your crops. Similarly, if you have a lot of data, ensure you protect it from attacks and disasters by maintaining a backup. Do this routinely and store the backups on encrypted disks on a different network altogether.

Ensure that backup devices do not operate using the same login credentials as other devices. Create and maintain different passwords for backups so that attackers cannot crack them easily.

Security Training

Create training routines for your teams and teach them the best security practices. A small fifteen-twenty minute training video on subjects such as phishing, spoofing, social engineering, etc. can help employees learn about various types of cyberattacks.

Office 365

If your organization uses Office 365, make sure to check out the Office 365 Secure Score tool. The tool goes through the active settings and configurations to generate a security score for you. Based on the security score, it also gives you suggestions on what you need to do to get a better security score. A better security score indicates that your network and tools are secure.

G-Suite

Many businesses today use G-Suite for email solutions. Google has placed all security measures in place, so it triggers a notification every time it sees unusual activity happening on any of your accounts. For example, log in through a different device or IP address.

Continuous Evolution

It is important for every business, regardless of whether it is a big or small organization, to learn more about the latest cybersecurity practices and newly emerging threats in the information world. Therefore, keep your business and employees updated about security policies, hardware, and software related to your organization.

With all these settings and configurations in place for your business, you will have a better grip on your business infrastructure. That way, you can effectively identify a potential threat when you experience an attack or even before you have been hit.

Some Tips to Maintain Cybersecurity

This section lists some tips to help you maintain cybersecurity in your personal systems. This chapter helps you understand how businesses can maintain network and application security.

Hackers Will Target You

You cannot pretend that a hacker may never attack your system or network. You must remember that every individual is at risk, and the stakes are always high. A hack can harm your personal and financial wellbeing, and ruin your reputation or even the business. Thus, cybersecurity is every individual's responsibility. Follow the tips mentioned in the book and remain vigilant. You must do your part to protect yourself, the business, and others.

Always update the software when you install any software or applications on your system. Always remember that the programs and operating systems are critical to management. You must install the security updates for all software and applications on your device. All you must do is turn on the automatic updates feature in the application, so the updates are automatically downloaded onto your system. Ensure that you update your browsers and any plug-ins.

Be Wary of Phishing Scams

As mentioned earlier, a phishing scam is a threat, and attackers may use various social engineering techniques to trick you into providing personal and sensitive information that can lead to both personal and financial losses. We also discussed the different types of phishing scams that attackers can perform. Always be suspicious about any email message or phone call where they ask you for too much information. If you are unsure about what to do when you receive phishing emails or messages, refer to the earlier chapters to learn more about them.

Always Maintain Strong Passwords

Every user has many passwords to use and manage, and it is always easy to take some shortcuts. Some users reuse their old passwords, and this is a very unwise thing to do. Password management programs help you maintain unique and distinct passwords across different accounts. If you do not know what type of password to maintain, use these tools to generate strong passwords. These applications may also remind you to update your passwords periodically.

Watch what You Click

Do not visit unknown websites, and never download any software or application from these sources unless you know what they are for. These websites host malware and are automatically installed on your system when you download the application. If you find the link or attachment suspicious or unexpected, you should not click on it.

Do Not Leave Devices Unattended

Technical security is one aspect of your devices, but there is also physical security that you must consider. When you leave your phone, tablet, or laptop in a public space without locking it, anybody can access the information on those devices. If you protect data on an external hard drive or flash drive, you must ensure it is locked and encrypted. Always lock the screen of your desktop or laptop when you do not use it.

You must understand that security experts can only do so much. If you do not help them protect the systems and network, there is no way the business is safe. The attacker can hack the system and obtain the necessary information.

Use the tips mentioned in this chapter to prevent any attacks caused due to your mistakes.

Chapter Eight: Web Application and Smartphone Security

The previous chapter looked at how organizations can secure their systems and networks. But is this enough? Or is there a need for more? Where does the process of security end exactly? Advancement in technology has led to the development of web applications. Today, most businesses have web applications, and many also use the cloud to store data securely. The demands of customers have evolved since the inception of modern Web 2.0 and web applications based on HTML5. Customers want to access data and information whenever they want. All these demands have put pressure on businesses to move their data onto web applications and cloud. For example, banking and shopping operations have moved online. You no longer have to walk into a bank or supermarket physically.

This has made life convenient for customers as they can do things at the comfort of their couch, but it has some drawbacks. This has increased the number of cyberattacks or attempts that hackers make. This led to the introduction of another chapter in the security domain known as Web Application Security.

This chapter looks at web application security, some myths around it, and how businesses can use web application firewalls to keep attackers away from their business.

Web Application Security

A web application firewall or WAF is a security protocol that works at the application level to filter HTTP and HTTPS traffic, thereby providing security from attackers at the application layer. In simple words, if an attacker tries to exploit a known vulnerability in a web application, it can block such attacks and protect the website or application from an attack. However, there are some cons to this process.

Here are some of the drawbacks:

It can only detect known vulnerabilities

A web application firewall has certain rules configured in its settings. It matches the web traffic rules and classifies the application based on whether the traffic matched with those rules or not. Given this, a web application firewall cannot protect you against newly discovered vulnerability in the web application. However, web application firewalls are effective against denial of service attacks.

It is only as good as its administrator

A web application firewall has rules configured by a user. This means it is only as good as the weakest link in the chain and the user who configured the firewall. It is difficult to determine if there are any issues within the system. Therefore, if an experienced user does not configure the web application, it can be completely useless.

Does not fix security issues in a web application

A web application does not automatically fix its code, and you must understand that. So, if there are loopholes in the application, it can only protect those loopholes from the attacker's eyes based on the configured rules. The code still needs to be fixed by a human developer.

A web application firewall is a normal application and has its vulnerabilities

A web application firewall is a software, like any other application, open to security issues. There are instances where attackers obtained admin access to the web application firewall through vulnerability and turned it off. They also break into the application firewall.

Thus, web application firewalls are an additional layer of security but not the end solution. It is good practice to have a web application firewall (WAF) for an application, but if budget permits, it is always good to apply additional layers of security.

It is important to pay attention to the vulnerabilities in the system or web application and fix them irrespective of the presence of a web application firewall. Businesses should have web application vulnerability testing as an integral part of their product quality testing processes.

How Can You Secure Web Applications?

To understand if the web application is completely secure, you must identify vulnerabilities in the system before an attacker finds out and starts exploiting them. You should test a web application for vulnerabilities during the entire software development life cycle and not only when the application goes live.

There are various methods to test a web application for vulnerabilities. You can use any of the following methods:

- Use a black box scanner to scan the web application.
- Use a white box scanner to detect issues with the application code automatically.
- Manually audit the source code of the application.
- Do a manual penetration test and security audit.

You cannot use just one method to test the system's vulnerabilities since no method can guarantee a 100 percent detection rate. Every method has its pros and cons.

For example, an automated tool can discover almost all vulnerabilities concerning code compared to a manual tester, but it cannot detect any logical loopholes. The tool cannot think like an attacker and will have an underlying code or application to perform the test. Manual intervention is required to identify logical flaws in the code. Conversely, it can take a lot of time, effort, and money to identify technical loopholes manually, and you cannot guarantee that the manual tester has identified all vulnerabilities in the system.

It is advisable to use every tool available to test a web application if there is no time and budget constraint, but this only happens in an ideal scenario. Therefore, realistically speaking, a business needs to choose the most effective solution regarding time and money to simulate an attack. Most businesses use a black box scanner known as a web vulnerability scanner. It goes without saying that a manual audit should follow an automated web vulnerability scanner. This ensures that both technical and logical vulnerabilities are identified.

Web Vulnerability Scanners

Black Box scanners, also known as web vulnerability scanners, are automated applications that scan websites and web applications for vulnerabilities and other security issues. Web vulnerability scanners became popular because they are easy to use and automate the whole scanning process. If you use a white box scanner, you need to access the underlying code and take the help of someone who understands application development. But with black box scanners, anyone with minimal technical knowledge can operate the web vulnerability scanner and test a web application.

How do you choose the correct web vulnerability scanner?

The Internet is full of web vulnerability scanners, both for commercial and non-commercial users. It is difficult to choose a scanner that works best for you. Therefore, you must test every scanner available to understand which one suits your application. You must consider multiple aspects before you choose a web vulnerability scanner. The first and obvious question is whether to use a free scanner or one with a commercially paid license? It is recommended that you always use a commercial scanner since they have regular updates, enable support from professionally trained teams, etc.

You can then choose a web vulnerability scanner based on the following criteria.

How well can it identify web application attack surfaces?

When you test the scanner, carefully examine what one has the best crawler. A crawler is a scanner component, which scans the application for all entry points where the attacker can initiate the hack. It is a critical component since it is easier to identify vulnerability only when the entry points are identified.

To understand what crawler is the best, analyze the results given by each crawler. Use the following parameters:

1. The number of pages scanned

2. The number of files used

3. Various parameters included during the scan

There is a possibility that a crawler was unable to scan the entire surface of the web application. This often happens when the crawler must be configured manually, which brings leads to the next point.

User-Friendliness of the Web Vulnerability Scanner

While most black box scanners are automatically configured to scan a web application, some may need you to specify certain parameters manually. Your business does not need to have a dedicated web application security team to configure a web vulnerability scanner as per business requirements. This means that the security scanner should be user-friendly so that anybody with basic programming or technical skills can configure the scanner. User-friendly web vulnerability scanners help businesses save money since they do not have to hire specialists to work on it.

Ability to Identify Vulnerabilities

The next criterion is to see which web vulnerability scanners can identify the maximum vulnerabilities and how many contain false positives. Web vulnerability scanners find thousands of vulnerabilities in a web application, but more than 60 percent of those were false positives.

You may ask why this is a problem? The issue with false positives is that a manual auditor must spend more time trying to verify if the vulnerability is indeed a vulnerability. This is a waste of resources and, therefore, needs to be avoided.

Automation

More automation in a web vulnerability scanner is equal to more relief for the company. This means that a tester need not manually configure each parameter since the scanner is already configured to scan well-known vulnerabilities. There are more vulnerabilities in a web application than what meets the eye. It is practically impossible for people to identify every vulnerability even if there is a time restriction. It is safer to use an automated scanner since it can complete the scan and identify vulnerabilities within two-three hours.

Additionally, a tester's knowledge about any vulnerability in the system is dependent on their experience. An automated web vulnerability scanner is already equipped with knowledge of existing vulnerabilities in web applications, and the developers of that scanner constantly update the database based on newly discovered vulnerabilities in different web applications.

In addition to these technical steps that you can take to secure your web application, you must stay informed. The Internet is full of information with blogs and websites on web application security. You can protect your applications and software better if you update your knowledge and skills regularly and stay abreast of what is going on in the industry.

Smartphone Security

When someone talks about a ransomware attack, people immediately think of attacks on employees using laptops or desktops. This is where an attacker thinks differently. An attacker always considers all possibilities that help them enter the system or network. An easy way to do this is through smartphones, which are easy to hack into and offer quick rewards.

The following are some numbers concerning cybercrimes and smartphones:

- Reports suggest that the number of attacks on smartphones had gone up by 50 percent in 2019 as compared to 2018. This was not just for Android devices. There is an estimate that, presently, around 1.6 million attack campaigns are targeting Apple devices.

- Reports by the researcher Ponemon suggest that in the past twelve months, 67 percent of small-medium sized businesses are victims of cyberattacks, and 58 percent were victims of a data breach. All this because of inefficient security on smartphones.

- The data breach report presented by Verizon in 2019 showed that 42 percent of the victims were small business owners.

- Forty-seven percent of small-medium sized businesses agreed that they do not know how to secure smartphones to protect their businesses.

Attacking smartphones is getting popular since attackers always look for new ways to attack your business. For instance, even state-sponsored attacks have started integrating smartphones to gather information for their attacks. The reason smartphones are targeted is because everyone takes smartphone security for granted.

Here are the simplest ways users and business owners can protect their smartphones and data:

Update the Operating System and Apps

Just like you would do in the case of your laptop or desktop, it is also important to keep your smartphone's operating system and its applications up to date. Many people are idle about updating their smartphone's operating system and apps. This opens their smartphone up to new vulnerabilities. When operating system and application providers roll out an update, they try to patch any discovered vulnerabilities. For instance, when OnePlus decides to upgrade the system, it sends you a notification. Once you download and install it, it tells you what fixes it made to your phone. Application providers also do the same. There may be a weekly update at times. If you do not update your smartphone, it becomes an easy target for attackers.

Today, businesses also have a Bring Your Own Device BYOD policy where personal smartphones can be connected to the office network. This being said, businesses need to train their employees about the importance of keeping their smartphones up to date.

Lock Your Smartphone

Keeping your phone unlocked is convenient for checking texts, emails, etc., but imagine if you forgot your phone in a coffee shop. What do you think will happen? If you do not have a security code, anybody can pick your phone up and access all your information. If your phone contains business information, you will put your business or organization at risk because of minor negligence.

Therefore, always make it a point to lock your smartphone with a passcode or biometric authentication.

Use Inbuilt Device Security Features

You can use the "locate my device" feature if you misplaced your smartphone. The feature makes your phone ring, which can threaten the thief or help you locate your phone if you lost it temporarily.

There are options on the phone even to delete all data if there were a few incorrect passcode attempts.

Using Bluetooth and Wi-Fi Wisely

Many people like to use free or public Wi-Fi. If you are using a smartphone with critical business data, think twice before you do this. Make it a point to ensure that the Wi-Fi you use is from a legitimate network. Free Wi-Fi available across public spaces such as coffee shops, malls, etc. are less secure.

The same goes for Bluetooth. People tend to ignore the Bluetooth feature leaving it on all the time. An attacker can take advantage of this ignorance, and break into your phone if they get sufficiently close to you.

App Permissions

When you install an app on your smartphone, it asks you permission to access certain features on your phone. Be careful before you approve these permissions. For example, it is understood for Google maps to have permission to access your location since it needs this to give you the right information. On the other hand, if a simple game you downloaded asks you for permission for your location, you need to be alert immediately. For all you know, attackers created the game to access your location. An application may ask many other permissions, so make sure to read these permissions before you give the application access.

Phishing and Spam Emails

Your smartphone also has an email application, and therefore, hackers can use phishing to obtain sensitive information. Thus, everything you learned in Chapter Three holds for emails received on your smartphone.

Data Backups

Data backups are as important for your smartphone as for your laptops and desktops. Some issues may occur at any time. Your smartphone may get stolen, or you may cause accidental damage to it. Therefore, it is advised that you maintain data backup.

Smartphone providers these days even offer automated backups for your data through cloud services such as Google Drive for Android and iCloud for iPhones. Always take advantage of this feature, so you never have to worry about losing your data.

Antivirus Apps

It is good to have an antivirus app installed on your smartphone since it protects your phone from any kind of malware. Attackers always deploy malware first to your device, and so it is best to install an antivirus app to prevent any attacks.

Source of Your Apps

The majority of users ignore this fact, but it is very important that the apps you download come from trusted sources. For Android, the Play-store is a trusted source, and for Apple, the app store. There are certain apps unavailable on the play store or app store, and this is due to security reasons. Users tend to sideload these apps that may be tampered with by an attacker, and your smartphone is conveniently opened up for attack just because of your negligence to sideload third-party apps.

To conclude, smartphones are critical extensions to business, more now than ever, and are no longer just a device used for making phone calls. Given its form factor, you can easily lose it, or it can be robbed. Therefore, it is really important in the modern world to care about the security of your smartphone just as much as you care about your other devices.

Chapter Nine: 9 Security Testing Methods

This chapter looks at the different types of security testing methods. At the end, it will focus more on penetration testing. Most organizations adopt this form of testing to identify any vulnerability in the system and network.

The business maintains cybersecurity testing measures are kept in place to check how prepared they are for any potential attack. A business may have an internal testing team or outsource the security testing to an external team when the need for security testing arises.

Attackers are relentless when they want to perform the attack, and they always look for new loopholes in the system. There are methods such as Penetration Testing, User Awareness testing, Red Team Assessment, etc., that help businesses scan through their infrastructure for loopholes that are otherwise overlooked.

Types of Security Testing

Vulnerability Assessment

The method of vulnerability testing is employed when a business needs to identify drawbacks within their systems, applications, and networks across their infrastructure. The following assets can be reviewed by implementing vulnerability testing:

- Web Applications
- System Builds
- Network Devices
- Network Infrastructure
- Phishing Attack Surfaces
- Mobile Apps

User Awareness Testing

User Awareness Testing, also known as UAT, is when business users test the routine tasks on an application. A business is built on its employees, but as mentioned, they can also be the weakest link to the security of a business process. By implementing user awareness tests and simulating attacks, a business can determine how employees react to a certain kind of attack.

User awareness testing has proved to be effective in identifying both digital and physical vulnerabilities. It helps you understand the level of preparedness against a phishing attack, and what a business can do to educate its employees regarding cybersecurity.

Red Team Assessment

Attackers do not follow any rules, and they do as they please. They know how to use different tools and software to attack the system and network of an organization to steal sensitive information. They may also find a way to disrupt essential services. A Red Team Assessment test helps the organization determine how prepared it is for any attack.

This test covers every attack surface, internal or external, and considers the application layer, network layer, employee awareness, and the physical aspects of security. The test is conducted legally with all required authorizations and uses harmless attack vectors to break into the infrastructure and exploit it in all ways possible.

Members of a red team assessment usually check the following entities for exploits and vulnerabilities.

Physical

Tests check for vulnerabilities at the physical level, such as the office, data centers, warehouses, and other relevant buildings.

Technology

Tests cover all the digital infrastructure. The team also tests personal BYOD and official mobile devices and other network devices such as routers, switches, etc.

People

Tests check internal employees, external contractors, business partners, and other high-risk departments.

After the assessment is completed, a detailed report is created and presented to the management. The management then consults with various cybersecurity experts in the organization to take preventive measures and improve the infrastructure.

Build Review

Build Reviews are tests performed by a dedicated team of security professionals on software every time a new version is rolled out. Build reviews help the organization perform a thorough assessment of every new software build. This helps the team strengthen the software's security further through a feedback loop, ensuring that it is safe from an attack.

The following components are tested as a part of build reviews:

- Servers
- Firewalls
- Active Directory
- Switches
- Routers
- Database Servers

- Application Servers
- Workstations

Penetration Testing

Most organizations adopt this method extensively to address the security concerns of the organization. This section takes you through the process of penetration testing.

Penetration Testing is the process of testing applications to find vulnerabilities. The teams do this by bombarding the network with malicious vectors after prior authorization from a business. The organization simulates an attack similar to a real attack to identify any vulnerability in all surface areas of digital infrastructure.

The purpose of penetration testing is to find any loopholes in a system and patch them before an attacker can access the system without authorization and steal sensitive information.

A penetration test is also known as a pen test and an ethical hacker. It helps determine if the existing defense mechanisms of a system are sufficient to prevent any attacks. Furthermore, there are reports generated after the completion of a penetration test that tell the business what countermeasures they must add to the system and network to prevent any attacks.

A system may have vulnerabilities due to the following reasons:

Error During Design and Development

Nothing is ever perfect, and there are chances of flaws in both software and hardware. The presence of the smallest of errors in software design can expose critical data during an attack.

Bad System Configuration

This can be another reason why there are vulnerabilities in the system. Poorly configured systems may open a backdoor for the attacker to break into the system and steal or destroy data.

Human Errors

There are multiple errors a human can make when they develop the application. They may also make silly mistakes, such as leaving the system unlocked, poor coding of software, leaving the desk and documents unattended, falling prey to phishing scams, etc., which can result in security breaches.

Complexity

The vulnerability of a system is directly proportional to the complexity of the system. An attacker is likely to find more surfaces for attack if the system has many features.

Connectivity

It becomes child's play for an attacker to break into a system connected to an unsecured or open network.

Passwords

The utility of a password is to prevent unauthorized access to something. Passwords need to be complex to avoid random guessing. Organizations must develop a robust password policy. It is also important to change your password regularly and not share them with anyone. These are the basics of securing a password, but despite this, people still share their passwords or write them down on paper and forget about it, and use weak passwords.

Inputs from Users

You may have heard of terms such as buffer overflow, SQL injection, etc. Users give different inputs when they use an application, and a hacker can use these input systems to harm the system.

Management

There is a lot of cost and effort involved in managing the security of systems. If the organization does not have a proper process in place to manage risk, the systems will be vulnerable and easy for a hacker to attack.

Insufficient Training

When the organization does not train its employees and other technical staff, it can cause some errors.

Communication

Communication channels, such as the Internet, mobile networks, telephones, have opened up new media for attacks.

Penetration Testing Tools and Providers

There are automated tools available in today's market to help you identify standard vulnerabilities. Pen test tools scan code to see if any malicious code lines can result in a security breach. They also validate encryption techniques and find any loopholes in the system or network. Additionally, they also test for hardcoded values in code, such as the username and password.

You should consider certain criteria before selecting a penetration testing tool. They should at least satisfy the following requirements:

- They should be user-friendly and, therefore, easy to use, configure, and deploy.
- They should be able to scan your system irrespective of how complex it is.
- The reports generated by the tool should be able to classify the threats based on severity level. This will help you prioritize your fixes.
- It should be capable of verifying vulnerabilities automatically.
- It should also re-verify any exploits found in the past scans.
- The tools should be able to do detailed logging and reporting.

Once you narrow down the kind of tests your infrastructure requires, you can train internal employees or external consultants to use these security tools. The following is a set of known tools used in penetration testing worldwide.

Nmap

Nmap is an open-source tool. It is used to scan a network and retrieve information about a network. Simply put, Nmap makes use of IP packets to gain information about the following:

- The number of hosts available on a network
- The services offered by those hosts
- The operating system of the hosts
- The firewalls used by the hosts
- And lots of other important information

It is supported on all operating systems and was originally developed for mass scanning of networks, but it works well on single hosts too.

Wireshark

Wireshark is again a free tool used to analyze networks. It gives you a microscopic view of the network's activities and is therefore used extensively by businesses, governments, and educational institutions.

Acunetix

Acunetix is a penetration testing tool used by software engineers and security professionals since it has numerous features. It is user-friendly, robust, and straightforward. In addition to using internal tools, a business may also directly outsource its penetration testing to leading security companies, some of which are mentioned below.

ScienceSoft

ScienceSoft is a recognized company in the information technology domain for its software services. However, it also takes an interest in providing cybersecurity solutions to companies. The company has been on the market for seventeen years and is experienced in all penetration testing methods, namely, white box, black box, and grey box. This company can test small, medium, and large businesses.

You can contact the cybersecurity team of ScienceSoft to get any assistance in setting up a penetration test for your business.

ImmuniWeb

Based out of Geneva, Switzerland, ImmuniWeb is another well-known penetration testing company. Their penetration testing platform boasts of a DevSecOps feature, which combines people and artificial intelligence to test the system. It also commits to a zero false-positive SLA. Additionally, they also claim they have detected the highest number of vulnerabilities detected and effective reporting. They have a comprehensive set of tools for penetration testing and also include APIs, IoT devices, mobile, and web testing, etc.

They have the following key features:

- Detection of new code in a continuous fashion.
- Manual testing at affordable pricing.
- Patching with single clicks.
- 24/7 support.
- CI/CD integrations for DevSecOps.
- Instant integration.
- Multi-resource dashboard.

Why Penetration Testing?

You may be wondering why this chapter is focusing more on penetration testing. The WannaCry ransomware that hit the world in 2017 has already been discussed. It was responsible for locking out more than two lakh users out of their computers and demanded money to unlock the systems. It affected many businesses around the world. Penetration testing could have helped these businesses prevent this magnitude of an attack since these tests, when conducted regularly, report the loopholes in security.

Penetration testing majorly helps with the following scenarios:

- Securing user data.
- Identifying vulnerabilities in an application.
- Determining the impact on business in case of a successful attack.
- Helping a business meet compliance concerning security.
- Many IT clients have started asking for penetration tests to be included in the software release life cycle.
- Much financial data is transferred between systems today, and it needs to be secured.

User data is the biggest currency in the world, and loss of such data can cause monetary and reputation damage to an organization. For instance, picture someone hacking a social media website like Facebook, hacking its user database, and exposing those details publicly on the Internet. Facebook can face legal consequences if that ever happened. Therefore, many businesses now enroll for compliance certifications before making financial transactions through their websites.

Some of these compliance certifications include:

- PCI DSS (Payment Card Industry Data Security Standard)
- ISO/IEC 27002, OSSTMM (The Open Source Security Testing Methodology Manual)
- OWASP (Open Web Application Security Project)

Types of Penetration Testing

Social Engineering Test

Social Engineering has already been detailed in Chapter Six, so you already know that social engineering attacks are executed to trick people into disclosing sensitive information about themselves or their organization. Thus, humans can be the weakest link in a security system.

Social engineering tests are conducted by emulating a social engineering attack. An employee is called via phone or contacted via a medium like text or email, and a scenario is put forward to try and test if the employee ends up disclosing any information. If the test is positive, it will be documented, and steps will be taken to educate employees about it.

Web Application Test

As discussed, various software tools are used to test how secure the code of a web application is. They test the code for any vulnerability and find a way to patch them to prevent any attacks. The team performing this test writes a report that discloses the flaws, and the development team can fix them as soon as possible.

Physical Penetration Test

Many organizations have physical devices on their property and must ensure that only authorized personnel can access the stored devices. This is more so in government and military facilities. All network-related devices and physical entry points are tested for any vulnerabilities. This test is not very relevant to software testing as such.

Network Firmware Testing

Networks are the most important part of an organization's digital infrastructure. Therefore, tests are conducted on all the entry points of a network, and these tests check the traffic going in and out of the point. This test can be conducted both locally and remotely.

Client-Side Testing

During these tests, the organization tests the software on the client's infrastructure to identify any vulnerability in the system.

Wireless Network Testing

As the name suggests, this test will scan all the Wi-Fi hotspots in an organization for vulnerabilities.

The Penetration Testing Lifecycle

The organization follows a disciplined process when it conducts a penetration test. Here is the process:

Data Collection

The first stage of a penetration testing life cycle is the collection of data. Penetration testers use numerous methods to collect information on the target system. The methods may use either a simple or complex tool or application to collect the data. Pen testers may also inspect the source code of the website to gather data about the target system. Simply put, any information about the target system available publicly is useful and documented. There are several paid and free tools available that the organization can use to collect information about the target system.

Vulnerability Assessment

The data collected in the first stage is analyzed and used to identify the target system's weaknesses. Penetration testers now attack specific attack surfaces to identify any vulnerability. They may conduct these tests using trial and error.

Exploitation

Based on the information collected in the first and second stages, the hackers can use different tools to access the system and exploit it. The exploit could be of any type. A penetration tester may steal data, modify it, or destroy it. Given this is an ethical test, data is usually never destroyed as the tests are conducted against production servers.

Maintaining Access

The next stage is about maintaining access. A hacker does not exploit a system repeatedly since it may trigger the alarm. So, they usually access the system or network once and then deploy tools to maintain their connection to the target system. A penetration tester needs to cover this possibility and emulate the different ways an attacker can maintain access to the system so that they can patch those loopholes.

Reporting

The final stage of the penetration testing life cycle is reporting. Extensive and detailed reports are to be created of tests performed, vulnerabilities found, and steps the organization can take to patch these vulnerabilities. The team must present the report to the senior management of the company, describing the tests and assessments carried out. This report helps the management understand the priority of infrastructure security and invest the required time, effort, and money to secure the business against an actual attack.

To conclude, security testing is a mandatory part of a software delivery life cycle, and organizations should never neglect this process. It costs a bit but definitely helps the business secure its assets against high-level cybercrimes.

Chapter Ten: Skills Required for a Career in Cybersecurity

You are nearing the end of this book, and thus far, you have learned a lot about cybersecurity. So, what next? It is good to have all this knowledge, but what should you do if you wanted to use it? This chapter looks at the careers available in cybersecurity and the skills you need to develop to pursue such a career. The classification of the roles in this chapter will help you decide what area you would like to work in.

A career in cybersecurity is not a bed of roses; it can be stressful. However, it has its rewards. Cybersecurity professionals find themselves in different roles across the organization, but their objective remains the same. They must develop methods and tools to protect the organization's data from any attack.

The process of getting into a cybersecurity role in the industry is not always straightforward. Some people jump into it right out of college, while others like to get some experience in software engineering before choosing to move to a role focused more on security.

Here are some career options available in the cybersecurity field based on the experience of the candidate:

Entry-Level Roles

- Systems Administrator
- Systems Engineer
- Web Developer
- IT Technician
- Network Engineer
- Security Specialist
- Mid-Level Roles
- Security Analyst
- Security Technician
- Incident Analyst
- Cyber Security Consultant
- IT Auditor
- Penetration Tester

Senior Level Roles

- Cyber Security Architect
- Cyber Security Manager
- Cyber Security Engineer
- Chief Information Security Officer

Four Popular Careers in Cybersecurity and How to Get There

Security Architect

If you like to solve problems, and develop strategies to prevent the same problems, consider the role of a security architect.

A security architect is responsible for designing, developing, and implementing security for an organization's systems and networks. They are capable of developing efficient complex security structures. The security structures can prevent any malware, DDoS, and other attacks.

The average salary for a security architect in the USA is around $120,000 per annum. Security architects must have at least five years of experience in the IT industry and three to five years in security.

Follow the path given below if you wish to pursue a career as a security architect:

- Pursue a degree in information technology, computer science, cybersecurity, or any other relevant field. Alternatively, you can earn equivalent industry-level certifications.

- Enter the industry as a systems administrator, security administrator, or network administrator.

- Work in the same organization for a while, and move up the organization until you reach a security engineer level.

- At this point, you can switch to a security architect role.

The responsibilities of a security architect are as follows:

- Research about current attack trends and design security architecture for all IT projects of the business.

- Provide the requirement to management for networks and network devices.

- Perform security testing, such as risk analysis and vulnerability testing.
- Research about the latest standards in security and implement them in the organization.

Training

The role of a security architect is a senior-level role, and therefore recruiting managers to look for specific certifications when they hire any candidate. Industry-level certifications in cybersecurity give your profile an edge over your competitors. You can first earn a CompTIA Security+ certificate and then proceed to the Certified Ethical Hacker (CEH) certification.

To move on to the advanced and expert levels, you can earn an EC-Council Certified Security Analyst (ECSA) certification and Certified Information Systems Security Professional (CISSP) certification.

Security Consultant

A security consultant, also known as a cybersecurity expert, knows everything there is to know about cybersecurity. They can analyze risks and problems and provide appropriate solutions to other organizations to secure their infrastructure and protect their data. Some organizations use a different name for this role. Some commonly used terms are security consultant, network security consultant, or database security consultant.

A security consultant is expected to be versatile and able to answer any queries related to cybersecurity. The salary range depends on the experience, but a senior-level security consultant can make up to $106,000 per annum in the USA. Most organizations prefer to hire consultants with at least three to five years of experience.

You can follow the path below to become a security consultant:

- Pursue a degree in information technology, computer science, cybersecurity, or any other relevant field. Alternatively, you can obtain the equivalent industry-level certifications.

- Enter the industry though a general IT role.

- Continue to work in the same organization and move up the ladder until you reach the security administrator, auditor, or analyst roles.

- Get yourself some industry-level certifications and improve your skills.

- Try moving to a security consultant role.

The daily tasks of a security consultant are as follows:

- Determine ways to protect systems, networks, and data from attacks.

- Perform security assessments and vulnerability tests.

- Communicate with staff and employees to understand security issues.

- Using industry-standard solutions to test security.

- Supervise and guide the security team of the organization.

Training

You can start with the CompTIA Security+ certificate and move on to the Certified Ethical Hacker (CEH) certification. You also need to earn the Cybersecurity Analyst (CySA+) certification.

Advanced certifications include Certified Information Systems Auditor (CISA), EC-Council Certified Security Analyst (ECSA), and Certified Information Security Manager (CISM). To get to the expert level, you can get certified with Certified Information Systems Security Professional (CISSP).

Ethical Hacker/Penetration Tester

Penetration testers, also known as ethical hackers, understand how an attacker thinks, and use that understanding to simulate different attacks on the organization's systems and network to prevent any malicious attacks. They perform this attack only with the management's consent, identifying the weak spots before an attacker can exploit them. This helps the business to protect their sensitive and critical data, both in storage and in transit.

The average salary of a penetration tester in the USA is $80,000 per annum.

If you want to become a penetration tester, follow the career path given below.

- Pursue a degree in information technology, computer science, cybersecurity, or any other relevant field. Alternatively, you can obtain the equivalent industry-level certifications.
- Enter the industry as a systems administrator, security administrator, or network administrator.
- Get yourself some industry-level certifications and sharpen your skills.
- Continue to work in the organization until you move up the organization and earn a senior penetration tester, security architect, or security consultant role.

The duties of a penetration tester are as follows.

- Conduct penetration tests on applications, systems, and networks.
- Analyze weaknesses to identify methods an attacker could use to exploit the system.
- Discuss and document the findings with the IT teams.
- Design and implement new tools for penetration testing to keep up with modern-day attacks.

Training

Start with the CompTIA Security+ and move on to the Certified Ethical Hacker (CEH) certification. At an advanced level, you can earn the CompTIA Advanced Security Practitioner (CASP) and EC-Council Certified Security Analyst (ECSA). To become an expert, you can earn the Certified Information Systems Security Professional (CISSP).

Chief Information Security Officer (CISO)

The Chief Information Security Officer profile is a senior-level profile in the field of cybersecurity. It is a very respected and rewarding job and includes a lot of power and freedom concerning creativity. The Chief Information Security Officer is responsible for assembling a security team and keeping a macroscopic view over the organization's security. The CISO will report to the CEO of the organization.

The average salary of a CISO is around $160,000 per annum in the USA. You must have at least seven to ten years of experience in the cybersecurity domain, and five years out of those must include managing security teams.

You can achieve the career level of a CISO by:

- Pursuing a bachelor's degree in information technology, computer science, cybersecurity, or any other relevant field. Alternatively, you can earn any equivalent industry-level certifications.
- Enter the industry as an analyst or a programmer.
- Continue to work in the organization until you move up the ladder to become an engineer, auditor, consultant, or security analyst.
- Get yourself some industry-level certifications and sharpen your skills.
- Try to become a manager of a team dealing with security.
- Get an MBA degree with a focus on IT.
- Get promoted to the role of Chief Information Security Officer (CISO).

You will be the head of the IT team, and your responsibilities will be as follows:

- Taking the last round of interviews to have the best team of IT security experts.

- Creating new plans for security project deployments and working on improving existing methods.
- Analyzing and approving the design and development of security policies proposed by the IT and security teams.
- Establishing programs for risk management by collaborating with other leaders in the organization.
- In the event of a breach, the CISO must take charge of the security teams and propose a plan of action to fix and prevent the breach in the future.

Training

When you start your journey off in the information security industry, you must obtain the Certified Information Systems Auditor (CISA). At the advanced level, obtain the Certified Information Security Manager (CISM) and become an expert by completing Certified Information System Security Professional (CISSP).

Required Skillset for a Career in Cybersecurity

Here are some skills that recruiters look for when they hire people from the cybersecurity industry.

Soft Skills

Leadership

A security expert leads a team through its ethics, credibility, and responsiveness. With amazing communication skills, a security expert can gain the trust and respect of senior management. It is also important to understand both the internal and external risks of the organization. Security leaders present all key information to the management and drive the business forward through informed decisions.

Always Learning

A security expert must keep up to date on the latest trends in attacks and solutions for those attacks. An aptitude for learning proves helpful for your personal and professional growth. Security is always evolving in the IT industry, and it requires someone who is a quick learner and can keep up.

Determination

The landscape of threat environments is always changing, and this demotivates some security experts easily. If you do not know how to tackle an attack, do not give up. Persevere and find a way to solve the issue. Determination and persistence always help you solve the issue. An ideal security expert always works on identifying a solution for any problem until the end and does not give up midway.

Collaboration

You must understand that cybersecurity is a shared responsibility of business. There are multiple teams involved, such as application developers, network engineers, server admins, management, and more. You must ensure you collaborate with every team in the organization and respect their inputs, as every input can be useful. Also, when you bond with stakeholders, you can explain the importance of and need for security. Ensure that every department in the organization does not ignore security.

Analytical and Insightful

A skilled security expert is good at analyzing incoming attacks and can assess how they can be thwarted. They further understand the attack surfaces and their vulnerabilities to minimize the attacks in the future. It can take a few years to develop this skillset, and sometimes it's also an intuition that helps a few individuals.

Hyper Critical Thought Process

A skillful security expert knows how the attacker thinks. This helps them visualize how the attacker may plan and execute the attack.

Therefore, they know how to think like the attacker and conduct penetration tests to identify vulnerabilities in the system before the attacker uses them to exploit the system and network.

Approachable

A security expert has to communicate with other teams constantly. Sometimes other teams may even want to consult the security expert before making changes to network policies or code. Thus, you must be approachable so that other leaders and team members can consult you. The combined effort helps the business strengthen its network and security policies.

Project Manager

Since you are a cybersecurity leader, you work day in and day out to protect your organization against attacks. You must develop holistic solutions rather than going with a solution for every attack module.

Technical Skills

Incident Management and Response

As a security expert, you are expected to handle any threat that violates the organization's security in real-time. There could be an incident involving malware, phishing, ransomware, etc., and it is critical that you can handle the situation, resolve it, and prevent it from happening again.

SIEM Management

SIEM stands for Security Information and Event Management. There are tools and services part of SIEM, and a security expert is expected to be well versed with them. You must learn to automate security procedures using SIEM tools so that the organization translates real-time alerts to response plans to prevent the effect.

Firewall

A security expert must thoroughly know the ins and outs of the firewall configuration so that it becomes easier to filter out malicious traffic from the network. Additionally, they must be very knowledgeable about intrusion detection and intrusion prevention systems and how they could be used in combination with the firewall.

Intrusion Detection

You are expected to know the workings of the intrusion detection system thoroughly so you can leverage it against any attack.

Application Security

A good security expert can find loopholes in the application and fix them before an attack comes in. It is also good practice to test applications during the software development life cycle to identify any vulnerability and fix them before deploying the application into production.

Malware Prevention

A good security expert can identify advanced persistent threats that may bypass traditional security solutions, such as firewalls, antivirus, etc.

Mobile Device Management

A security expert must work with the IT team to explain how hackers can exploit mobile devices such as smartphones, laptop, tablets, etc., to breach the system. They should further discuss how these devices could be secured to prevent a security breach.

Data Management

Data is the most expensive asset for any business, and a security expert should manage and protect it at all costs.

Digital Forensics

A security expert should know about digital forensics and leverage forensic tools to find anomalies in data or the network, which can be a backdoor for an attacker. They should subsequently patch the data or network if any anomalies are found.

Identity/Access Management

Through identity and access management, the organization creates roles, classifies users into groups, and then assigns roles to them. The IT team defines these roles along with the management, and a security expert is expected to audit the access levels granted to users and groups in the organization regularly.

Intelligence and Analytics

A security expert must know how to use analytics to understand historical attack patterns and learn how to predict future attacks and be ready for them. Reports suggest that if analytics is leveraged to combine network data and application data, it can help prevent attacks.

Audit and Compliance

While securing systems and networks, a security expert needs to ensure that all regulatory compliances such as PCI DSS, SOC, GDPR, HIPAA, PCAOB, SOX, etc., are adhered to by the organization. Compliance and security audits are critical since non-adherence to regulatory compliance can attract huge penalties or fines from the government.

Conclusion

Cybercrimes are happening every second on the Internet. Cybercriminals are constantly planning a crime, regardless of whether it is for monetary gains or to disrupt the peace of the digital world. Therefore, cybersecurity is more relevant than ever today. Businesses must protect themselves from various kinds of attacks that hackers can launch on their systems and network. Hopefully, upon completing this book, you have sufficient knowledge to protect yourself and your business from modern-day cybercrimes.

At the same time, this book might have inspired you to take up a career in cybersecurity. The demand for cybersecurity professionals has increased in the last few years since the number and types of cybercrimes have significantly increased. Recruiters in all industries find it very difficult to find the right talent for this job, and this gives anyone with the right skills and qualifications a huge opportunity. There is also a sense of urgency to fill these positions as cybercriminals are constantly planning a new attack and never take a holiday themselves.

This book has taken you through everything you need to know as a beginner in the cybersecurity domain and how to start planning if you want to take it up as a career. You have also learned enough to keep yourself protected on the Internet.

Here's another book by Quinn Kiser
that you might be interested in

COMPUTER
NETWORKING

An All-in-One Beginner's Guide to Understanding
Communications Systems, Network Security,
Internet Connections, Cybersecurity and Hacking

QUINN KISER

References

https://www.forcepoint.com/cyber-edu/cybersecurity

https://www.cisco.com/c/en/us/products/security/what-is-cybersecurity.html#~how-cybersecurity-works

https://www.cybintsolutions.com/20-cyber-security-terms-that-you-should-know/

https://list25.com/25-biggest-cyber-attacks-in-history/

https://www.varonis.com/blog/cybersecurity-careers/

https://www.newhorizons.com/article/4-cybersecurity-career-paths-and-the-training-to-get-you-there

https://cipher.com/blog/the-must-have-skill-sets-certifications-for-cyber-security-careers/

https://www.integrity360.com/cyber-security-testing

https://www.softwaretestinghelp.com/penetration-testing-guide/

https://www.netsparker.com/blog/web-security/getting-started-web-application-security/

https://www.zdnet.com/paid-content/article/protecting-your-mobiles-from-a-rise-in-cybersecurity-attacks/

https://www.businessnewsdaily.com/11197-protect-your-smartphone-from-hackers.html

https://www.forcepoint.com/cyber-edu/network-security

https://www.coxblue.com/how-to-protect-your-business-from-cyber-attacks-2/

https://www.tetradefense.com/cyber-risk-management/13-ways-to-protect-your-business-from-a-cyber-attack-in-2019/

https://security.berkeley.edu/resources/best-practices-how-to-articles/top-10-secure-computing-tips

Printed in Great Britain
by Amazon

27910533R00076